Shared and Collaborative Practice in Qualitative Inquiry

Shared and Collaborative Practice in Qualitative Inquiry: Tiny Revolutions is a short collection of reflections on ethical research practice and scholarly community. It explores the qualitative tradition through the process of writing, photography, dance, and narrative.

This is a book about ethical research practices, about simple truths, about the commitments we initially made to this work, and about how we might better support each other along the way. Most importantly, this is a book about finding and making our own communities. Communities do not belong to any one person or small group of people. Rather, communities—genuine, real, and vibrant communities—belong to us all. This is a book about how.

This book is suitable for people new to qualitative research and seasoned researchers who would like to explore and develop traditions in qualitative inquiry.

Jasmine Brooke Ulmer is an assistant professor at Wayne State University, where she directs the qualitative doctoral track in the College of Education.

Developing Traditions in Qualitative Inquiry
Series Editors: Jasmine Brooke Ulmer and James Salvo,
Wayne State University

The Developing Traditions in Qualitative Inquiry series invites scholars to share novel and innovative work in accessible ways, ways such that others might discover their own paths, too. In acknowledging who and what have respectively influenced our work along the way, this series encourages thoughtful engagements with approaches to inquiry—ones that are situated within ongoing scholarly conversations. Neither stuck in tradition nor unaware of it, volumes make new scholarly contributions to qualitative inquiry that attend to what's shared across disciplines and methodological approaches. By design, qualitative inquiry is a tradition of innovation in and of itself, one aimed at the target of justice.

From multiple perspectives and positionalities, concise volumes in this series (20,000 to 50,000 words) strengthen and grow the qualitative community by developing inquiry traditions as they should be developed: inclusively, diversely, and together.

For more information about the series or proposal guidelines, please write the Series Editors at jasmine.ulmer@wayne.edu and salvo@wayne.edu.

Volumes in this series include:

Shared and Collaborative Practice in Qualitative Inquiry
Tiny Revolutions
Jasmine Brooke Ulmer

Writing and Unrecognized Academic Labor
The Rejected Manuscript
James M. Salvo

For a full list of titles in this series, please visit: www.routledge.com/Developing-Traditions-in-Qualitative-Inquiry/book-series/DTQI

Shared and Collaborative Practice in Qualitative Inquiry

Tiny Revolutions

Jasmine Brooke Ulmer

Routledge
Taylor & Francis Group

LONDON AND NEW YORK

First published 2021
by Routledge
2 Park Square, Milton Park, Abingdon, Oxon OX14 4RN

and by Routledge
52 Vanderbilt Avenue, New York, NY 10017

Routledge is an imprint of the Taylor & Francis Group, an informa business

British Library Cataloguing-in-Publication Data
A catalogue record for this book is available from the British Library

Library of Congress Cataloging-in-Publication Data
A catalog record has been requested for this book

ISBN: 978-0-367-35579-1 (hbk)
ISBN: 978-0-429-34043-7 (ebk)

Typeset in Times New Roman
by Newgen Publishing UK

To James

Contents

List of figures   viii
Acknowledgements   ix
Preface   xi

1 Dear Reader: An ethics of authorship   1

2 Coming to terms   16

3 When the sun kisses the moon: A photographic
   interlude   31

4 Choreographing through chaos   34

5 Simple truths   53

6 Everyday invitations: A photographic interlude   63

7 Tiny revolutions   68

Coda   77
Index   79

Figures

0.1 *Hug*, 2018, Detroit, Michigan, USA   x
1.1 *Rotations*, 2018, Ghent, Belgium   13
3.1 *Arabesque 1,* 2018, Groningen, the Netherlands   31
3.2 *Arabesque 2,* 2018, Groningen, the Netherlands   31
3.3 *Arabesque 3,* 2018, Groningen, the Netherlands   32
3.4 *Arabesque 4,* 2018, Groningen, the Netherlands   33
5.1 *Beget,* 2018, New York City, New York, USA   59
6.1 *Unplug,* 2018, Groningen, the Netherlands   63
6.2 *Hope*, 2017, Detroit, Michigan, USA   64
6.3 *Welcome*, 2018, Leiden, the Netherlands   65
6.4 *Love,* 2017, Detroit, Michigan, USA   66
6.5 *Change,* 2017, Detroit, Michigan, USA   67
7.1 *Footprints*, 2017, Detroit, Michigan, USA   75

Acknowledgements

A book on shared and collaborative practice is not written alone. Given the series' focus on continuities, I would like to express gratitude to the many qualitative scholars who have shaped my work and created space for the writing that appears here, including those who reviewed the initial set of book and series proposals.

This book was made possible by a 2017–2018 Wayne State University Humanities Center faculty fellowship on the topic of revolution. It was also made possible by a pre-tenure sabbatical with support from my program, college, and university, as well as support from my awesome methodological colleagues, Barry Markman and Shlomo Sawilowsky. I am also grateful for opportunity to spend several months as a visiting scholar at the University of Ghent.

This book was also made possible by Routledge. Thank you to Una McGovern for wonderful copyediting and to Amy Kirkham and Matt Bickerton for seeing this book through. Indescribable thanks are due to Hannah Shakespeare for not only supporting this book and this series, but for being a wonderful person. Hannah, you are a beacon of light. I am appreciative that *Shared and Collaborative Practice* will be a companion piece to *Writing & Unrecognized Academic Labor.*

I am forever grateful to James Salvo, the best kind of personal and professional partner.

Figure 0.1 Hug, 2018, Detroit, Michigan, USA.

Preface

Uncertain times

It is difficult, nowadays, to know what to do or where to begin.

It has been this way for quite some time now, even before the world suddenly changed. When I started this book, I had hoped that—in some small way—this book might respond to the ways in which humans have relentlessly been inflicting violence on each other and on the earth. As I finish this book, I find myself writing from one of the early epicenters of an event that is already being described as Pandemic 1—an event in which long-standing disparities continue to be made more visible each and every day. I struggle for words amidst a silence punctuated only by the surveillance of circling helicopters and the sirens of ambulances making one-way trips. Unimaginable loss has already arrived. Worse, on so many levels, it seems here to stay.

I am not sure precisely how or what one is supposed to write in the middle of a pandemic, and I apologize for places where I have missed the mark. I recognize that what I wrote before may read differently mid- and post-pandemic, particularly as we search to recognize ourselves in this rapidly changing world. I had finished the manuscript before this all occurred, and although I had been planning to do one last round of revisions to smooth out the text, I've since decided to leave it as is. What follows from this point forward are words I wrote when we lived in a different world than the one we live in now—words written for an Anthropocene in which humanity might still have ten more years to create meaningful change. I'll let those words remain in place as a marker for what was on the chance that any of it might still be useful for what still might be.

* * * * *

It is easy to feel small, powerless, and unable to spark any sort of change. Being only one person among billions can seem overwhelming indeed.

So much is completely beyond our control. There are only a limited set of decisions that people are able to make in life, generally speaking. Given the circumstances, however, there are even fewer decisions that folks will be able to make from here. Of the choices that remain, one involves whether or not we choose to engage in a shared and collaborative practice—of whether or not we are committed to the people in our lives, to the people on this planet, and to the other forms of life on Earth.

As such, this is a book about survival in the face of mass extinctions, including those of the academic type. This is a book about ethical research practices, about simple truths, about the commitments we initially made to this work, and about how we might better support each other along the way. Most importantly, this is a book about finding and making our own communities. Communities do not belong to any one person or small group of people. Rather, communities—genuine, real, and vibrant communities—belong to us all. This is a book about how.

Like the series that it's part of, this is also a book that seeks to promote positive continuities in qualitative inquiry. Much has happened since the field initially came about, and it's important to share what has already been learned. At the same time, the field is continuing to expand across disciplines as it develops new inquiry traditions, and it is my hope that future generations of scholars will have opportunities to do this still. There is much worth continuing. Yet, in writing this, I would be clear from the onset that simply because some ideas and practices have existed does not mean that they should continue to exist in the same way, or even that they should be continued at all.

As vital as some continuities are, there are some ideas and movements that decidedly should *not* be continued. This is the case in research, in life, and anywhere else they might occur. Racism, sexism, classism, ableism, ageism, colonialism, homophobia, transphobia, xenophobia, and religious discrimination are among them, as are violence, hate, ecological destruction, and genocide. Not a single one of these ideas needs to be furthered, as they never should have existed in the first place. Conversely, there are ideas that we should keep exploring. The continuity of nonviolent revolution, collaboration, and sharing are among them. So are hope, love, conviction, and faith in the potential of others and ourselves—we will also need to selectively continue these in order to continue living.

And while it is difficult, if not impossible, to predict what might happen from here or how we should respond, a recent passage from educational theorist Michael Peters gives me pause. As Peters writes,

Anthropogenic extinction is seen as a strong probability during this century based on the threat of nuclear annihilation, biological warfare, pandemic, overpopulation, ecological collapse, climate change, AI technology ('superintelligence') and geological or cosmological disaster. Many contemporary scientists, including microbiologist Frank Fenner, Stephen Hawking, and climate change scientists who, for example, warn that humans are unlikely to survive the existential climate-related security risk thirty years into the future. Ray Kurzweil, Google's chief engineer, suggests that life as we know it will cease by 2045.[1]

These are issues that, for many theorists and philosophers, invoke not only matters of life and death, but question whether or not life will even continue. Some cut straight to the chase. Audre Lorde, for example, encourages futures for children that involve "thinking for survival of the species—thinking for life."[2] Others turn to the power of collective hope and imagination. "By choosing a different future," Gloria Anzaldúa writes, "we bring it into being."[3] Robin Kimmerer similarly suggests, "What we imagine, we can become."[4] The sense of urgency increases in intensity with each passing year, and the words that follow are written with this in mind.

The chapters in this book are intimately connected. At the same time, they also are meant to stand alone. So, what I would suggest is this: read a chapter. Maybe take a break. And, then, if you're still so inclined, please keep reading. That's all to say this might not be a book that is best consumed quickly, or even consumed in one sitting. Different chapters move in different ways.

Chapter 1 opens with a letter to readers. It shares the idea that continuity can be fostered through writing, as writing provides a point of connection through which to return. It is within this spirit that the chapter offers an ethics of authorship—one that treats scholars as real people. When we forget to treat people as people, we allow research to become even more dehumanizing than it already can be for everyone involved. Taking inspiration from communications ethics, this chapter builds the argument that, beginning with the ways in which we communicate with each other, we must move along relational axes of community in order to thrive and survive.

Chapter 2 continues to highlight the need for shared and collaborative practices in qualitative inquiry. With an emphasis on how sharing and collaboration have developed in the Anthropocene, this chapter attempts to come to terms with several concepts that we have and need today. After engaging with the crowd-sourced dictionaries and family texts that were shared with me, the chapter then turns to the concept album, *Miss Anthropocene*, by Grimes.

Chapter 3 offers a brief photographic interlude. The choreographic images of the dancer, stenciled in as street art, repeat again and again. The images are from the Netherlands, and were located in and around Groningen. This interlude serves to transition into the next chapter, which takes up revolution through dance. It primarily does so through the music and choreography of Hofesh Schechter in the production *In Your Rooms*, as it was performed at the Opera Ballet Vlaanderen in Ghent, Belgium.

More specifically, Chapter 4 considers how choreography can help us deal with chaos. Beginning with the question of what it means to be human, this chapter moves with the concept of revolution, observing that we are always in motion, even when life seems to be holding us still. Approaching revolution in this way can help us to focus on what matters most, even, and especially, in uncertain times. This is what Hofesh Schechter accomplished in *In Your Rooms* and what Alvin Ailey accomplished in *Revelations* before that. Read alongside each other, these choreographic works explore not only how dance brings people together within a shared and collaborative practice, but how dance can bring some of the simplest human truths to bear.

From there, Chapter 5 advocates for return to simple truths in research. The first part of the chapter, which draws from remarks on a panel concerning post-truth in research, takes up the idea that love is a simple truth, is a shared truth, and perhaps is the simplest of revolutionary truths. The second part of the chapter attends to several of the difficult truths facing us as qualitative inquirers today. By way of response, Chapter 6 then offers a photographic interlude. The images of street art pictured here address the topics of belonging, love, hope, and change. Most of the photographs in this interlude are from Detroit, Michigan. All are from my archives.

Chapter 7 closes, or reopens, if you will, with a question for us all: *and if, then how*? If we are to continue as members of an academic community, and if we are to continue as members of humanity beyond that, this is a question we must all ask ourselves.

As a researcher, I believe that scholars are best positioned to contribute to a better world through research. As a methodologist, I believe that methodology profoundly shapes how we are able to proceed. As an inquirer, in some small part, I hope this might be a tiny part of how.

Notes

1 Peters, "The Armageddon Club," 2.
2 Lorde , *Sister Outsider*, 78.
3 Anzaldúa, *Light in the Dark/Luz en el Oscuro*, 21.
4 Kimmerer, *Braiding Sweetgrass*, 184.

References

Anzaldúa, Gloria E. *Light in the Dark/Luz in el Oscuro: Rewriting Identity, Spirituality, Reality.* Edited by AnaLouise Keating. Duke UP, 2015.
Kimmerer, Robin. *Braiding Sweetgrass: Indigenous Wisdom, Scientific Knowledge, and the Teachings of Plants.* Milkweed Editions, 2013.
Lorde, Audre. *Sister Outsider: Essays and Speeches.* Random House, 1984.
Peters, Michael A. "The Armageddon Club: Education for the Future of Humanity." *Educational Philosophy and Theory*, advance online publication, 2019.

1 Dear Reader

An ethics of authorship

Because ethical inquiry involves people treating each other as people, I would note that the writing in this book is to you, from me.

I should share, however, that this is more of an address than it is a dedication. For as often as scholarship is described as a form of conversation, it often seems as though scholarship isn't written *to* anyone at all. Nor, at times, does it seem like it's been written *from* someone. Yet, writing does not magically appear. Whether it's everyday writing, scholarly text, or fiction, writing comes from someone, somewhere, who is trying to accomplish something. This is why we should work to make the practices of reading and writing explicitly clear. The ways in which we communicate matter.

This is especially important nowadays, as it's become very difficult to determine what's real and what's not. Some of the ways this can happen are more innocuous than others. It's not uncommon, for example, to filter and photoshop online photographs to hide a few extra pounds, some wrinkles, or both. We curate how we present ourselves to others, selectively choosing aspects of our lives to put on display, making visible what we want to make visible. Most of the time this seems innocent enough—when given the opportunity, why wouldn't we offer what we think is the best version of ourselves to the outside world? Why wouldn't we share pieces of who we are? It all seems harmless enough. Until, that is, the same platforms we use are weaponized by propaganda machines, are banished altogether, or are turned against us. Distorting, censoring, and misusing information are tools of geopolitical warfare just as much as they are forms of intimate control.

There are times when the truth of what's right in front of us is ugly. Sometimes the truth is difficult, but a world without truth is dangerous, so I'll get right to it. Although we now live in the Anthropocene—a suggested epoch that accounts for the ways in which humanity has become a geological force—we may not live beyond it. At the rate we're going, some scholars predict we won't. Humanity has been rapidly ushering in a mass extinction event with implications for, and also far beyond, our own species. In response, there has been a rare convergence of interests across disciplines as researchers and public scholars respond to the moment we find ourselves in. Many are now turning to scientific investigations, artistic endeavors, and philosophical theories to remedy and make sense of the hazards we face. Yet, as if attempting to undo what may be irreversible planetary damage is not challenging enough, those involved must also contend with deliberate misinformation campaigns.

One of the things that I would urgently suggest is that entertaining post-truth has been a serious mistake—one that has placed us in an even more perilous position when it comes to climate change. It is also a mistake that, in at least in some small part, has contributed to another rise of totalitarianism, authoritarianism, and fascism across the globe. At the same time—*and not unrelatedly*—several ethical and axiological imperatives in research have been forgotten. There are dangers in our midst, and they manifest in different ways. I'll come back to that, but before I do, I would note that the answer is not to withdraw into ourselves. If anything, we should share more—more of ourselves, our practices, our opportunities, our understandings. We should share more and collaborate with the world around us, and with the people around us, too.

For those of us who identify as qualitative scholars, the first imperative we can overlook involves the truth of people. This is deeply ironic, for as mindful as we can be about treating our study participants as people, we often fail to extend the same courtesy to ourselves. As readers and writers, however, we are people, too. It can be very easy, however, to keep writing into the abyss, unsure of who we are as authors, what it is that we're trying to say, how to take responsibility for how our work might be read, and toward what ends. When we forget these things, we overlook the potential of writing to bring us together in this present moment. Neglecting writing as a form of communication is thus a second imperative we forget. A third involves failing to maintain the historical threads of ideas, thoughts, and knowledge. It is necessary to recognize where our understandings of the world come from and how we should approach them differently over time. When we neglect to do any or all of these things, we become disconnected. Disconnected from truths that 1) there are people on either side of communication, 2) reading and writing are forms of communication that occur in the present, and 3) writing contributes to our historical trajectory.

Consequently, we become disconnected from the work we should be doing to make the world a better place; from our own selves as individuals; and from humanity and the planet as a whole. Forgetting these things is dangerous, too.

Over the last century, many authors have tried to convey the importance of remembering to future generations. But in not heeding the caution George Orwell sent in 1949, for instance, his book *Nineteen Eighty-Four* came to foreshadow the return to where we are today: a time of deliberate propaganda tactics; political messages that are riddled with intentional ambiguities, contradictions, and outright lies; and governance by censorship, surveillance, and fear. In some places, we are not so far off from when the main character in this dystopian novel committed the act of writing, a thoughtcrime punishable by death. Orwell described his protagonist committing words to paper as such: "He was a lonely ghost uttering a truth that nobody would ever hear. But so long as he uttered it, in some obscure way the continuity was not broken."[1] This is my aim, too, in this essay, in this book, in this series, in the projects that will follow: to utter at least one truth that keeps continuity going, however mundane or apparent it might seem. The most important truths bear repeating, especially in uncertain times.

Education should accomplish these things. It is, after all, intended to teach subsequent generations of young people the critical knowledge, understandings, and perspectives they need not only to survive, but to thrive. We are not at a point, though, where even *public* education consistently makes the world a better place by encouraging each and every person to reach their full potential in life as ethical and informed human beings. Though it should, in practice, all too often it does not. And now, the consequences of dismantling public education are coming into painful focus: as disinformation campaigns threaten democracy, we are experiencing significant environmental changes—changes that many, not uncoincidentally, deny. In these troubled times, crafting shared and collaborative accounts of where we have been, where we are now, and where we hope to go from here are as important as ever. There are—and there will continue to be—many ways to contribute. Ethical scholarship, archival projects, and creative works are but a few.

Futures without democracy are futures we should actively resist, as are futures involving human oppression, irreversible planetary damage, and unsurvivable climate change. It is within these spirits that I offer the theses below. The first stands alone as a point of emphasis; it is the cornerstone of this book and this series, and it will grow and be developed throughout both. Taken together, they are an attempt to make my aims in this book clear. It is my hope that each will invite conversations with those who share similar commitments.

Seven theses

1. Writing creates continuity.

2. Scholars are real people. It's an unusual thing to make this observation. And, yet, it might be helpful to mention this again, as this is something that's all too easy to bypass or forget. It can seem safer to detach and dissociate from our writings—to draw sharp distinctions between what we write and who we are. For when our writings are rejected, as inevitably happens either in part or in whole, it can feel as if *we* are being rejected. Similarly, when reviewers and readers tear our work apart, it can seem personal (and sometimes is). Writers may not *be* their writing, but they are connected to it. This is how writing can transform into a series of protective maneuvers and a defensive apparatus to hide behind. There can be something incredibly appealing within author functions that position the author as already dead.

I would suggest, however, that it can be helpful to consider the ways in which authors are very much alive. Even in writing this, I have situated myself as a real person who hopes to be in conversation with the other real people who might be kind enough to be reading this now. And maybe this is an odd thing to write, but I am real, and—whether or not I've had the opportunity to meet you—I would share my understanding that you, dear reader, are real, too. It is my hope that remembering that scholars are people might work to *rehumanize* and *repersonalize* academic reading and writing practices. This would provide several potential ways of moving forward, including approaching writing as a form of correspondence between and among people—which, in this particular moment, involves you and me.

This book is from me. I don't know when it is that you'll be reading this book or even who you are, but please know that it's from me. It's written from where I've been, what I'm thinking now, and where I hope we might go from here. It's also written from a woman from the Deep South who tries to live commitments to inclusive education through teaching, whether those involve classroom instruction or writing as a pedagogical practice.

I would risk stating what, postmodern theory aside, might be taken as painfully obvious: this book is written by me, as well. Though it might seem strange that I'm making a distinction between *from* me and *by* me, I would note that it is *from* me in the sense that the stories authors tell can, in general, be thought of as a gift to readers,[2] and it is *by* me in the sense that I am the author who wrote it. And while I'm not one to make anything all about me, I do feel it's important to be clear on these matters, especially in this post-truth era. Nowadays I prefer to deal in simple truths, myself, but that's another chapter. So, in the meantime, I would suggest that attending to the ethical dimensions of authorship is both timely and necessary.

Which reminds me, thank you for taking the time to read this.

This book is to you. I am still surprised, and very appreciative, when someone chooses to engage my work. I am reminded of when, in my first year as faculty member, a senior colleague paused in the hallway. When he remarked that one of the most rewarding parts of being a scholar is watching the texts we write take off on their own trajectories—sometimes taking on a life of their own—I paused, too. Truth be told, I hadn't thought about that before, although perhaps I should have. Up to that point, my strategy (if it could even be called that) had been to do the best writing that I could, move it through the publication process, list it on my c.v., forget it existed, and start the process all over again, abandoning many initial writings and full manuscripts along the way. I thought that once a text was released, its journey was finished (and for some of what I've written, that has been the case). It really hadn't occurred to me that when a text is published, it may only be at the beginning of its journey. It's not that I didn't take responsibility for what I wrote: it's just that I had a hard time imagining that anyone would ever choose to read it. Because life is short and there is always already too much to read, I try to write words that are a good use of your time. Please know that I know that I do not always succeed.

When I considered the title for this essay, I debated how to begin. Should I include everyone in advance with "Dear Readers" or follow the "Dear Reader" convention of epistolary novels, instead? The difference between plural and singular readership is subtle, yet important. For the most part, however many readers an academic text eventually garners, it tends to be read by only one reader at a time. Thus, our experience as readers is largely solitary, even for texts that end up being read by many people. And while I hope for multiple readers, when all is said and done, I am only certain that this text will have been engaged by one person (which would make the dedication of the book "to James" sadly prescient). We are now co-editors, but our partnership began with a letter. It was addressed to me in response to a published article I had authored—one I did not write to him, for him, or with him remotely in mind. I wrote an article,[3] he wrote a letter to me,[4] I wrote a letter back, and many letters later, here we are today. For us, scholarship has become an ongoing conversation, and my work continues to be better for it. All because I wrote an article that I didn't think anyone would read.

When I wrote that article, I was still writing into the void. It was almost as if taking a trip to the desert, walking out to the edge of a cliff, timidly whispering a manuscript out loud into a vast and empty canyon, waiting for a moment to see if anything would happen, and, after nothing did (or seemed to, anyway), turning around to go back home. For all intents and purposes, I was writing into the abyss. It took many years for anyone outside the editors handling my work or my closest group of friends (all of whom were either newly minted assistant professors or still graduate students themselves) to comment. I took the silence to mean one of two things, both of which I thought were negative: either my work was not being read because it was unremarkable, or, worse, it was too terrible to even acknowledge and people were just being polite by not saying anything. Having a better sense of the impossibility of reading all the excellent manuscripts that are published every day, I would take a more neutral stance now. But I didn't at that time, so instead I kept writing, hoping that perhaps the next piece might be better. That *it* might actually be worth reading.

What I've learned since then, however, is that reading and writing are social experiences, even though they are things that we most often experience alone. Even the event of other people reading our work can be a lonely experience. Though I wasn't aware yet, it is when I began to think about readers that my work began to be read. Whether we have readers yet or not, I've come to believe that when we read and write, we might do well to frame scholarship as something that has been written *by* someone *to* someone else. It simply makes for better writing. And, by and large, I think it makes for more enjoyable reading, too.

It's important, then, that we remember the human components of reading and writing. To only focus on reading and writing as if people are not on both ends ignores the human aspects of what we do. I wish I had realized this earlier. Perhaps, in what might have been an overemphasis on "writerly texts," I mistook Roland Barthes' concept of "readerly" for *readable*.[5] There isn't any shame in writing something other people can understand. Clear writing can be taken as a sign of clear thinking; I've often found that (and it's reverse) to be the case. That's not to say, though, that writing should be perfect: it never is. Nor will it ever be. That's okay, and we should be gracious as readers and writers and accept that as a given. We should also take the time to honor those who will read our work by not pushing incomplete writing (and, by proxy, incomplete thinking) out the door too soon; our time is better spent emphasizing quality over quantity, which is something we value in this line of inquiry. Further, we are smart and skillful enough to take on the challenge of conveying difficult, complex, and even chaotic ideas without alienating those who sincerely want to engage our work.

For someone to give us the time and grace of readership is a gift to us, too. Thus, writing clearly is not a limitation that forecloses upon every possible literary convention in advance; it is an opportunity to convey what we think is most important in this world while doing the work we most passionately believe ought to be done. If we have something that is truly that important to say, then we should want as many people to understand it as possible. In any event, I have found that readable texts are significantly more challenging to write than texts that aspire to be writerly. Having something to say and saying it clearly are much more difficult than they initially seem.

This is not to imply that every piece of writing we generate needs to take epistolary form or break the fourth wall to directly address readers. What we can do, however, is think of others when we compose and make considered efforts to repersonalize the acts of reading and writing. *For we can't, in one breath, decry the ways that this process dehumanizes us as scholars and, in the next, voluntarily give away our humanity as authors.*

3. Scholars are more than author-functions. Contemporary accountability systems want us to complete our designated functions, and productively at that. While claiming otherwise—whispering sweet nothings to each drone that they, in fact, are the one true queen—accountability systems want each tired worker bee to keep adding more cells to the honeycomb; they want the indistinguishable "I's" to contribute more and more palatable writings—one sweet argument at a time. When we forgo the humanity in what we do and forget the people involved, we're co-opted into furthering its aims as we risk transforming into algorithmic or neoliberal drones ourselves. And when we further erase ourselves by writing texts without authors or readers, we subscribe to hive mentality and co-opt ourselves once more. It didn't help Prince avoid exploitation when he turned himself into a symbol, and it won't help us, either. This is even how attempts to resist can end up serving that which we are trying to avoid; without realizing it, we construct our modes of resistance within frames that would hold us still, losing ourselves in the process and ultimately serving interests other than our own.

4. Scholars can reclaim their humanity by writing through an ethics of authorship. Dehumanizing is a word that is used all too often to refer to the processes, experiences, and institutions involved in producing scholarship.[6] As partial remedy, I outline how the qualities of an ethics of authorship within qualitative inquiry might respond. I would begin by noting that

An ethics of authorship differs from an ethics of scholarly writing. Both are needed. When we teach the ethics of scholarly writing, we tend to begin with a few general rules: do not plagiarize, do not take ideas in peer review and later present them as your own, be sure to acknowledge contributors, cite sources properly... these tend to be the principles we start with first. We also spend time teaching students the ethical importance of how we portray participants, how we include co-researchers, and which stories we do and do not tell. According to our disciplinary style manuals and guides, these are all elements that are entailed within the ethics of scholarly writing. They are necessary.

The ethics of *authorship*, however, is something slightly different. Whereas the former involves standard procedural guidance and representational concerns, the latter involves commitments to not only an ongoing critical practice, but to authors as people.

An ethics of authorship involves writing as ourselves and encouraging others to do the same. One of the most distinct affordances of qualitative inquiry is that authors are often encouraged to write as their own selves. When this is possible, it shouldn't be wasted. Whether it's the voice of an individual author, a collaborative pairing, or a larger collective, texts that feature what we're most passionate about are wonderful; they are a treat for readers and writers alike. This is what initially drew me to qualitative inquiry: alongside its neighboring disciplines, qualitative inquiry was interesting, informative, and enjoyable to read. As a graduate student, I'd sit on the floor in between library stacks and read, pulling books off the shelves until I reached the limits of what my dust allergies would allow. Well-known to many others, but new to me, what I found was captivating. I went author by author, starting with the first of what they'd written and moving through the last. As I did this, I read through lifetimes of work. Sure, I read other things, too, but I kept returning to the corners of qualitative inquiry. Exploring the many possibilities for what it was and what it could still yet be, and I appreciated how the authors I read brought qualitative inquiry to life.[7] And though the experience was special to me, I'm not alone in the joy of finding new authors.[8] When I began attending conferences later on, like many others, I wanted to hear the unique cadences, the intonations of the words I spent so much time with. I wanted to see, to listen, to hear. I wanted to know how to read authors' words as if they were right there with me, reading out loud. I still do.

The authors who I appreciate most are the ones who most attend to the craft of writing, even though they take up writing in many different forms. From stories and autoethnographies to theoretical readings, creative multimodalities, interpretive findings, essays, and more, qualitative inquirers write lives, thoughts, learnings. They convey questions and performances, observations and knowledges. They write with kindness, and they write because they have something to say. They share through the sorts of technical manuscripts that are central to any discipline—the sorts that work toward collective understandings and goals. They also communicate lamentations and fears and regrets and moments of pure joy while also giving thought to how to do it differently all over again. And, when they do this, they share something of themselves that is *special*. For this, I am grateful. Strong writing always stands out across aesthetics and styles. It's my belief, at least, that when we write, regardless of which genre(s) we are writing within, we end up leaving fingerprints all over our work. It's best, I think, when those fingerprints are mostly our own.

Which brings me back to the ethics of writing as our own selves. When we *don't* do this outside technical contexts, it may be because someone is discouraging us, we're choosing not to, or we don't yet know how. Everyone starts somewhere, and that's more than okay, for writing evolves over the course of a lifetime. In other words, writing is a practice: it takes time, effort, and patience to figure out where to write and how to use writing as vehicle for expression, especially when we are still trying to find ourselves as people and develop as scholarly thinkers. It's difficult, after all, to write as ourselves when we don't yet have a strong sense of who we are, how we think, and what's important to us. And even if and when we do, writing as ourselves potentially puts us in an uncomfortable position—one that makes us vulnerable.

Although it might seem safer to emulate someone else than risk letting others see who we really are and how we really think, imitating others mostly forces us to write from a differently uncomfortable position, as if we are wearing someone else's clothes while pretending otherwise. Mentor texts can be helpful at the beginning of one's trajectory, especially when it comes to learning how to converse and situate one's own work within the very real nuances of academic discourse communities. And though no one ever truly writes or thinks in isolation, of course—and very little, if anything, is truly ever new—we should not simply replicate what others have already done. When we prevent our own practices from developing, we limit not only our own potential, but the potential impact of our work. Being that we have so much to give, we owe it to ourselves and those around us to keep trying. Why is that? Because as qualitative inquirers, we have the capacity to influence the world by being our whole selves, sharing what we have to offer, and collaborating widely so that others can do the same. We should take advantage of this possibility in ways that enhance each of the respective projects in which we are involved.

The most helpful advice I've come across was posted online by Gloria Ladson-Billings several years ago. I'm paraphrasing here, but the gist of it was this: *don't worry about being the next someone else. Be the first you.* That's powerful advice, and it's something we should all do. We should all give ourselves the grace, permission, and freedom to discover what it sounds like when we write as ourselves and let others do the same. Not to mention, we write most effectively when we write from our own perspectives and positionalities. Or, put differently, we write most effectively when we write as people. That's as important as ever nowadays.

An ethics of authorship approaches authors as people. Anytime we write, we write with at least some degree of vulnerability. And the more of ourselves with which we write, the more vulnerable we can be. For some authors and authors-yet-to-be, this can be frightening. In this respect, what an ethics of authorship instead might do is to help us grow and develop together in sustaining, humanizing ways by

- writing how we would want to be written about;
- citing how we would want to be cited; and
- reading how we would want to be read.

No one person already knows everything or knows how to do everything perfectly in a way that is pleasing to all people at all times. In addition, everyone makes mistakes and has room to grow, and our scholarship is a place where the limitations of even our very best thinking can show. It's undesirable to write in a culture of fear, and when we create academic cultures in which scholars are too afraid to write, we risk missing out on what may be some of the most interesting thinking.

An ethics of authorship takes authorship seriously. In parts of the world without free speech, writing can be a crime punishable by imprisonment, exile, torture, and death. Those of us with this privilege should not approach it lightly. Though we shouldn't take ourselves too seriously in the process, we *should* take the privilege of authorship seriously: for ourselves, for other authors, and for the authors who will follow. This means opening spaces up rather than closing them off. It means not filling space in publications because we can, but because we have something useful to say. It means challenging ourselves to do our best thinking every time we write. Taking authorship seriously involves taking responsibility for what we write, using opportunities wisely, and preserving intellectual spaces for subsequent generation of scholars. Our actions today will influence the futures of scholars in our fields, as our actions will influence whether or not our fields will continue to exist. I very much hope they will.

An ethics of authorship encourages us to read and write together as a scholarly community. As a scholarly community, we live in different parts of the globe. We work in different fields and disciplines and all have different gifts to offer. And we already have many strengths: we're smart, well-read, resourceful, creative, and, together, we know how to do a lot of things. We're also stronger than we think, both as individuals and as collective scholars. When I imagine how much greater our shared impact would be if we helped one another, I am overwhelmed with possibilities. Because there are many spaces to be in and many resources to be shared, together, we can operate as stewards of our disciplines who are mindful of what it is that we're passing on. This brings me to the fifth thesis.

5. Our work should support the next generations. We do not have to wait to meet our future colleagues. We can begin this work, and should, with young people now. Children and youth are smart and capable, too. There is much we can learn from young people by listening to them, especially when it comes to the truths that children already know. Often, I would venture, they can be more clear-headed and insightful than adults on exactly what matters most in this world. This capacity is fortuitous, for we will have left young people no choice but to use it. Our futures— as a community, as a species, as a planet—will depend upon how the next generations of young people adapt to an immensely different world from the one into which we were born, raised, and taught to consume. A world we created, but the consequences of which they will live. Children who sense we're on the brink of environmental catastrophe are already beginning to ask how we could allow this to happen. Their questions will only continue to grow.

We need to partner with future generations of children through communications and education, and we need to do this now. This is of the utmost importance, for if we don't educate our children, those seeking to undermine democracy will. Authoritarians want us to believe we have no futures, no pasts—nothing but this present moment in time. And while a focus on the present might seem appealing in an immediate gratification sort of way, it is short-sighted in both directions. Children are neither born with an innate sense of history nor with speculative visions of futures yet-to-come. The present is simply how it is—there is no reason for children to believe that there ever were, or that there could ever be, different ways to live. This leaves future generations of young people highly vulnerable to exploitation by adults who won't live long enough to fully experience the effects of their selfishness and greed. When we do not allow our children to have concepts of the future or historical memories of the past, we deny our children agency, initiative, and choice. Children are people, too, and our children deserve better than this.

If we hope to foster a radically inclusive, welcoming world—a world that is built on sharing—then we must learn to live in other ways. Ways that help us look beyond ourselves in support of others, ways that creatively leverage the best of what we have to offer, ways that work toward better futures for us all. And thus,

6. We must move along axes of community, together, in order to thrive and survive. The imperatives we face as scholars in community with one another are perhaps not so different from the imperatives we face as members of this planet. We are in the midst of at least one, if not more, mass extinction events. In response, whether it's in scholarship or everyday life, I agree that we must learn to live in ways that foster a shared world and cultivate life.[9] We must work toward being human as a form of praxis.[10] We must work toward decolonized, geosocial futures[11] that work against the proliferation of inequalities.[12] We must hope and act[13] and assemble in intersectional ways,[14] and we must work toward futures that are plural[15] and inclusive.[16] We must do these things for children, for adults, for plants and animals and air and water and soil and everything and everyone else. It is rapidly becoming clear that if anyone or anything is to survive, let alone thrive, then it will take working together along inclusive axes of community—ones that have yet to be realized.

Before continuing, though, I would add just one more thing. It's a thesis, yes, but it's also a belief, a necessary hope, and a vision for what it is we all can do.

Figure 1.1 Rotations, 2018, Ghent, Belgium.

7. We can all learn to live in a world continued by shared and collaborative practices. You may be wondering how. To be fair, this is something that I often wonder, as well. And when I do, I return to the same line of thought: though we may feel small with respect to what we can accomplish alone, what we can achieve collectively is impressively large. In the Anthropocene, and in any epoch, really, we owe it to each other to try.

Sweeping changes stem from tiny revolutions.

Notes

1 Orwell, *Nineteen Eighty-four*, 28.
2 Kimmerer, *Braiding Sweetgrass*, 347.
3 Ulmer, "Writing Slow Ontology."
4 Salvo, "Slow Reading," 7.
5 Barthes, *S/Z*, 4.
6 See Paris and Winn, *Humanizing Research*.
7 Ulmer, "Writing as Gratitude," 819.
8 Bridges-Rhoads et. al, "Readings that Rock our Worlds," 817–837.
9 Irigaray, *To Be Born*, 89.
10 McKittrick, "Yours in the Intellectual Struggle," 3.
11 Yusoff, *A Billion Black Anthropocenes or None*, 61.
12 Latour, *Down to Earth*, 2.
13 Badiou, *I Know There Are So Many of You*, 62.
14 Butler, *Notes Toward a Performative Theory of Assembly*, 26.
15 Nordstrom, "Plural Pasts, Presents, and Futures," n.p.; c.f., Mouffe, *Agonistics*, 8.
16 See Evans-Winters and Esposito, "Researching the Bridge Called Our Backs."

References

Badiou, Alain. *I Know There Are So Many of You.* 2017. Translated by Susan Spitzer, Polity, 2019.
Barthes, Roland. *S/Z.* 1970. Translated by Richard Miller, Hill and Wang, 1974.
Bridges-Rhoads, Sarah, Hilary E. Hughes, and Jessica Van Cleave. "Readings that Rock our Worlds." *Qualitative Inquiry*, vol. 24, no. 10, 2019, pp. 817–837.
Butler, Judith. *Notes Toward a Performative Theory of Assembly.* Harvard UP, 2015.
Evans-Winters, Venus, and Jennifer Esposito. "Researching the Bridge Called Our Backs: The Invisibility of 'Us' in Qualitative Communities." *International Journal of Qualitative Studies in Education*, vol. 31, no. 9, 2018, pp. 863–876.
Irigaray, Luce. *To Be Born: Genesis of a New Human Being.* Palgrave Macmillan, 2017.

Kimmerer, Robin. *Braiding Sweetgrass: Indigenous Wisdom, Scientific Knowledge, and the Teachings of Plants*. Milkweed Editions, 2013.

Latour, Bruno. *Down to Earth: Politics in the New Climactic Regime*. Polity, 2018.

McKittrick, Katherine. "Yours in the Intellectual Struggle: Sylvia Wynter and the Realization of Living." In *Sylvia Wynter: On Being Human as Praxis*, edited by Katherine McKittrick, Duke UP, 2015, pp. 1–8.

Mouffe, Chantel. *Agonistics: Thinking the World Politically*. Verso, 2013.

Nordstrom, Susan Naomi. "Plural Pasts, Presents, and Futures of Post-Qualitative Inquiry: Two Questions for the Field." *Qualitative Inquiry*, advance online publication, 2020.

Orwell, George. *Nineteen Eighty-four*. Harcourt Brace, 1949.

Paris, Django, and Maisha T. Winn, editors. *Humanizing Research: Decolonizing Qualitative Inquiry with Youth and Communities*. Sage, 2014.

Salvo, James. "Slow Reading: Reflections on Jasmine Ulmer's 'Writing Slow Ontology.'" *Qualitative Inquiry*, advance online publication, 2018.

Ulmer, Jasmine Brooke. "Writing as Gratitude." In "Readings that Rock our Worlds," edited by Sarah Bridges-Rhoads, Hilary E. Hughes, and Jessica Van Cleave. *Qualitative Inquiry*, vol. 24, no. 10, 2018, pp. 819.

——. "Writing Slow Ontology." *Qualitative Inquiry*, vol. 23, no. 3, 201–211.

Yusoff, Kathryn. *A Billion Black Anthropocenes or None*. University of Minnesota Press, 2018.

2 Coming to terms

To know where we're going, we have to know where we've been. And when and where we've been, as the last chapter addressed, is living in the Anthropocene. We live within uncertain times, and we're still developing the language not only to describe it, but to respond.

However much we might wish it otherwise, no one person will be able to save the world, because no one person ever saves anything alone. No one successfully takes on something of that magnitude by themselves, whether the work involves scholarly inquiry, planetary life, or both. When it comes to major projects, even on occasions when only one person's name is listed, many other people are most likely involved. For example, though a director may receive recognition for the film, everyone in the credits (that we sometimes fail to watch) had a part in making it, too.

It's easy, though, to believe in the myth of the singular hero. Lasting works of art have been built around this idea: from Odysseus and Aeneas to Luke Skywalker and Captain Kirk, the heroes we imagine are designed to bring us escape, protection, and relief. Yet, as tempting as it is to believe in allegorical heroes, they don't exist—at least not in the way we construct them. The bad news is that we can't rely on just one person to save us from our troubles; but, on the flip side, it also means that we are relieved of the burden of having to be that person ourselves. It is not necessary, nor is it desirable, to try and be a saviour.[1] Plus, it's not even possible.

If and when there are things we want to accomplish, what we can realistically do, instead, is work together. What we can do is share.

Please share nicely

Many folks were taught from a young age to share, including me. And not just to share, but to share nicely at that. I heard this from my mother, I heard this in school, and then, later on, I said it to countless schoolchildren myself: *Please share nicely.* As much as we may have heard this as children, though, this is something that, as adults, we can be apt to forget. It is easier to share things that have already been placed in front of us: toys, books, crayons, markers, turns swinging on the swings or sliding down the slides. Those weren't ours to begin with. We didn't have to make them, build them, buy them. If and when those items were available, they just appeared. So, when we did have things to share as children, we were really just sharing things that other people had already chosen to share with us.

This is worth remembering across the lifespan: when we are able to share, it is likely because somehow, somewhere, at some point down the line, someone shared something with us. Probably many someones sharing many somethings. Further, the most important things we have to share are immaterial, such as time, space, knowledge, compassion, understanding, hope, love, forgiveness, insights, opportunities, and faith. These can be shared, too, and we shouldn't lose sight of them. If we've had the joy of experiencing these, we might understand that each are gifts that others chose to give to us and we, in turn, chose to receive. Each are ways of sharing nicely.

Sharing nicely, however, implies that there are other ways to share, some of which are not so nice. There's a poem in *The Light in the Attic*, authored by Shel Silverstein, that's helpful here. It's called, "Prayer of the Selfish Child," and it's a parody of the classic children's prayer, "Now I Lay Me Down to Sleep." In many of the classic versions, children pray for angels to watch over them. In this version, however, should the children die before they wake, they "pray the Lord my toys to break."[2] What Silverstein is suggesting is this: some children are so averse to sharing that, in principle, they would prevent others from having access to "their" things, even if those things are no longer of any use to them. They feel a need not only to hoard toys for themselves, but to keep toys away from others. Regardless of whether or not they even have any interest left in those toys, they'll still use everything up just so that no one else can have any.

I'm of the opinion that ways of sharing that aren't nice aren't within the spirit of sharing, so I keep with definitions that involve kindness, unselfishness, and consideration, instead. I do so, in part, as I describe below, with the help of what was shared with me.

Family heirlooms

It was located in a house that I entered through the carport only rarely. Carefully stepping across the tiny green lizards scattering in every direction, into the house, away from the heat, and out of my shoes, my bare feet were greeted by hundreds of small, cold, white, hexagonal tiles. They bordered the shag carpet that, after living most of its lifetime in avocado green, later transformed into an unexpectedly electric shade of lime. Its dye competed in citric intensity with the grapefruit and tangelo trees outside.

I usually spent my time, though, on the other side of the shag carpet in the Florida room. The room smelled warm, perhaps because the sliding glass door kept all the cool air on the other side. In it, there were many soft-but-scratchy things: curtains, indoor-outdoor carpet, a broom, a less-than-comfortable pull-out couch. The couch was across from a wall containing the record of all of the grandchildren's heights, marked in pencil in each visit along with our names, our ages, and the date. Prominently displayed on a wooden pulpit on the other side of the room was a large dictionary.

Unlike most dictionaries today, the 1934 *Webster's New International Dictionary* was unabridged. At 20 pounds, it was heavy enough to need its own stand. My grandfather and I had at least one conversation about the dictionary, and it was because I asked why, of all the books he had, that one was special. I was about seven, and I don't recall all the details, but the basic outline of what he wanted me to know was this: reading is a path to knowledge, and knowledge is a form of power that is available to anyone who can read, including people with less access to formal education. When we can access texts and look up words and concepts we don't know yet, he said, nothing is unavailable to us—nothing is unavailable to anyone. He bought the dictionary as a younger man because reading was, and still is, a radically democratizing force.

It was about two decades after that conversation that he passed. When our family gathered to clean out the house, his children decided I should be the caretaker of the dictionary. Because I would be returning to graduate school to begin a PhD program soon, they thought it should go to me. That, and his compact, two-volume version of the *Oxford English Dictionary*, or *OED*. I was honored, though I didn't think much of it at the time. I set them in a small pile, brought them 200 miles north, cleared space on the shelves, put them with the references, and then let them be.

They sat largely unopened for the next several years while I turned to an assortment of other things: random disciplinary dictionaries and encyclopedias, primary source materials, secondary texts, tertiary readings of the secondary texts supporting primary source materials, and so on. Only after the dictionaries continued north for another 1,000 miles, travelling past where my grandfather was born and raised, did I give them more consideration. Until then, I suppose, I had been concerned with shinier things, which is easy enough to do. But then I started to think about the invention of photography for a paper I was writing, how it evolved over time, and how photographs were initially conceptualized nearly two hundred years ago.[3] And I found myself searching for something deeper, something more.

Opening the family dictionary created shifts in my practice, including a renewed focus on what different practices produce. It had been a long time since I had meaningfully engaged reference materials. This may be nerdy to admit, but as a child, I enjoyed reading encyclopedias. I had a lot of questions about how the world worked, and the Internet was still a few years away from existing, so if I wanted to know something, the answer was most likely in a 22-volume *World Book Encyclopedia* set. I spent a lot of time sitting in front of the bookshelf reading. I had thought that made for an unusual childhood until, when James and I began writing letters to one another, it casually surfaced that we both read encyclopedias as children.[4] (At least I'm in good company.) That's all to say that even though it might sound a little strange, I do have meaningful connections to several reference works. That's also to say that I prefer to start with the family dictionaries, even if they aren't the perfect dictionaries and even though, like the references I've mentioned thus far, they've gone through multiple updates since.

I like the ritual of returning to these dictionaries. Of carefully retrieving 40 total pounds of books off the shelves, setting them down carefully on the floor, searching through the pages, and putting my face as close as possible to the tiny print, sincerely hoping the combination of a handheld magnifying glass with prescription eyeglasses will hold long enough for me to decode the impossibly small font.

There's something special about having references to return to, whether those involve entries that have fallen out of date or are emerging out of the zeitgeist into popular culture. I appreciate how *Merriam-Webster* does both nowadays through its online social media presence, bringing to the fore words and expressions that, often with a serving of timely shade, help us to understand democracy in real time. The ability to read and understand words is an important part of democracy, and, in keeping with democratic processes, it's something we should do together.

Shared vocabulary

Developing a shared vocabulary to understand the world together is a form of sharing—one that encourages inclusive participation and allows us to converse through shared terms. Given access and opportunity, we each have something to offer. Many somethings, in fact, and being able to contribute to a shared vocabulary is one of those things. When we are committed to doing so, it is possible to use vocabulary without contesting terms for the sake of contesting terms or pitting one language against another. Neither are productive moves. What we can do, however, is shift from competition to collaboration. We can shift away from using words as a different way to compete.

Though this unnecessary sense of competition arguably generates much of the conflict that arises in academia, conflict can also boil down to one party simply not understanding what the other party is trying to say. When we don't collaborate to create shared meaning because we're too busy trying to pull each other down, when we advance our own terminologies at the expense of others that may exist, and when we remain isolated in our self-contained bubbles, we risk creating further misunderstandings still. Concepts should help us, not be in the way.

Creating a shared vocabulary is one way to create shared meaning, and it takes many contributors, often collaborating over many generations, to make this happen. The ways in which multiple versions of the family dictionaries have been constructed are good examples of this, and they offer useful guidance when it comes to collaboration and sharing. I see in Webster's that to collaborate is "to labor together; to work or act jointly, as in writing or study."[5] I also see in the *OED* that to collaborate is "to work in conjunction with another or others, to co-operate; *esp.* in a literary or artistic production, or the like."[6] And I see that collaboration functions as a precursor to sharing in both.

The condensed version of the *OED* has no shortage of entries on sharing. In total, they take up almost an entire page,[7] which is even more impressive given that each page consists of four miniaturized pages from the full edition. This is where I should make a second confession regarding reference materials: when I reach my limit on deciphering the tiny font that sometimes begins to swim before my tired eyes, it's nice to open the online version of the *OED* in its place. Because the online version is a compilation of all the versions that have come before, it naturally repeats many descriptions in the condensed version. It's nice to know it's all still there. As such, I've listed several of my favorite definitions on sharing below:

- "To have a share (*in* something); to participate *in*, to take part *in*."
- "To participate in (an action, activity, opinion, feeling, or condition)."

- "To perform, enjoy, or suffer in common with others."
- "To possess (a quality) which other persons or things also have."
- "To receive, possess, or occupy together with others."[8]

The entries in *Webster's* run parallel with these ideas, with the succinct addition that to share is "to partake of, use, experience, or enjoy with others."[9] When multiple generations of reference materials are put together, it becomes clear that sharing is consistently portrayed as something we do with others.

Shareholders in humanity

Another form of sharing involves the notion that we each have, in this moment, about a one in eight billion share in humanity. This is the philosophical idea of distributive justice, and it follows a definition of "share" that is more along the lines of a shareholder (as in something that has been divvied up in which multiple entities have a stake). This approach to sharing is twofold: 1) as humans individually, we each have our own stake in humanity; 2) as humans collectively, our species lives alongside many millions of other species on Earth. As such, we are not only individual shareholders in humanity, we are *planetary shareholders*, too. And when we envision it all together, we can see that we are each part of something precious and unimaginably larger than ourselves.

So, whether we take the standpoint of humanity or planetary life, it might be tempting to state that we all are sharing in the effects of climate change and in extinctions already underway. However, this isn't quite correct, as both entail a form of sharing that, one, isn't nice, and two, isn't sharing. Moral philosopher Christine Korsgaard makes distinctions as to why. She writes,

> That word 'share' also embodies some assumptions. You don't share your secret with an eavesdropper, or your house with an intruder, or your land with a colonial oppressor, although in all of these cases he has it and you have it too. 'Share' suggests something more, that you have something together, that you both have it legitimately, that you have a common right to it.[10]

As Korsgaard is suggesting here, sharing is an intentional and reciprocal act. And many of the secondary environmental effects of climate change have neither been intentional nor reciprocal. Humanity has made a series of bad decisions about how to treat the planet, bad decisions that are compounded every single day, but I seriously doubt that many people, if any, get out of bed with the sole mission of annihilating the planet through the activities from which they profit. It is not so much an explicit desire to make the Earth hotter, for instance, as it is the continued, collective, and short-sighted privileging of selfishness, superiority, and greed.

The resulting long-term consequences will neither be distributed evenly nor fairly. Though no one will be able to fully escape the Anthropocene, there will be wide variations in how it is experienced. Elderly populations worldwide will be less able to withstand heatwaves, and it will be the same for children, too. Moreover, due to centuries of environmental racism, the Global South will experience the effects of climate change more severely than the Global North. Across the board, vulnerable populations will experience climate change disproportionally, as they will not only be among the first to be exposed to dangers but among the last to be granted relief. These things and others have been happening for a long time already. Environmental destruction and historical oppressions are inextricably linked. This is why feminist philosopher Nancy Tuana advocates for an ecologically-informed intersectionality, one that connects environmental exploitation with lineages of oppressions involving race, class, gender, sexuality, and more.[11] In so doing, Tuana implores us to attune to the layered and habituated ways in which some people and ecosystems are treated, wrongly, as disposable.[12] This is necessary for several reasons. It's morally just. And most importantly, it's the right thing to do. Beyond that, so long as anyone is treated as less-than-human, it will not be possible to remedy our more-than-human world.

If there is a premier example of not sharing, the Anthropocene might be it. This is an epoch that allocates resources to some yet not others, precludes a strong sense of togetherness, places boundaries on enjoyment, limits inclusive participation, and leads to suffering. Yet, due to the lineages of oppression that Tuana describes, it's not that everyone is actively participating in the creation of climate change so much as it is that some are having it done to them. And, as a result, those with privilege are positioned to lead a comfortable life at the expense of others who don't. Life is not something we have been set up to do or experience together in equitable, ethical, or meaningful ways in the Anthropocene. Not when it comes to democratic participation, emotional well-being, or general quality of life.

It didn't have to be this way, though, and it doesn't, still. It would be considerably more difficult to overlook the inequities that exist around us, for example, if we took an active and inclusive stance toward community. An emphasis on community offers a different path.

Shared communities

Communities are built on sharing. Communities are also, as Jean-Luc Nancy reminds us, the foundation of being.[13] These are threads that run throughout his contributions, and much of the most insightful thinking in continental philosophy on the topic of community comes from his works. In *Being Singular Plural*, he writes that "there is no meaning if meaning is not shared."[14] And in working to define sharing in *The Inoperative Community*, he observes that, "Sharing divides and shares itself: this is what it is to be in common."[15] These are a few of my favorite excerpts from his writings, and I have used them in conceptualizing this book.

The idea that "sharing divides and shares itself" is of particular interest here. It reminds me of a few things. It reminds me of how sharing is an action that can keep on giving, such as by pressing the "share" button on a particularly wonderful social media post; that sort of sharing can go on indefinitely, and it tends not to cost us much of anything. It also reminds me of a conversation I had with Brooke Hofsess about notions of scarcity in academia when she paused, thought about it, and said, "more is more." Sharing is an active process: it is something we can choose to do, and it is a way of knowing, living, and being. Sharing carries forward into a more desirable world.

So what does this mean with respect to the communities to which we belong, particularly academic communities? Further, what does this mean in the Anthropocene? We are in a moment in which the world as we know it is shifting, and academia is shifting with it. In many regards, we seem to be stretched beyond capacity on all fronts, with the ground literally disappearing beneath our feet. The other day I came across an article in the newspaper that opened with the following paragraph, and it struck me that it is all getting to be a lot to unpack. It began: "The record-high Great Lakes water levels are highly visual. Roads are crumbling, parks are flooded and closed, beaches have disappeared and homes are falling into the water."[16] The second and third paragraphs were not any more uplifting: "But the story of Michigan's high water problem doesn't end where the Great Lakes meet land. Inland communities, including those in mid-Michigan, are facing unprecedented conditions experts say could lead to widespread flooding."[17]

It is becoming clear that there is nowhere safe to go.[18] Solid ground is disappearing, and we are simply going to have to do the best we can to hold what remains together.

Some will be tempted to grab what they can, not look back, and rush to claim the last remaining bits of higher ground. But for those of us who stay either because we choose to do so or because there are no other options available to us, well, we will need a different plan. As I am urgently trying to express here, this plan will need to involve sharing. Sometimes these efforts will be small, such as uplifting our peers and fellow community members by pushing the "share" button to help increase the visibility of the good things they are hoping to accomplish. We can do the same thing with our citational practices, too, taking care to emphasize the work we believe ought to be shared so that others can benefit and partake. Citations are a way of sharing credit with the thinkers who contributed to the ideas that inspire our work. Imagine if we approached citations as tiny thank yous—as ways of highlighting the ideas with which we deeply engage. And imagine if we regularly used acknowledgement statements at the end of our writings to do the same, sharing a small amount of credit with those who were kind enough to assist behind the scenes. These are little things, and there will also be bigger and more important things before us. It's good to start practicing here, for what's ahead will be challenging, and we will need to share.

Creative collaborations within and beyond the academy offer a way to practice collectively coming to terms.

Creative collaborations

"The Anthropocene" may not have been in my grandfather's dictionaries or the encyclopedias I read as a kid, but it's a term that we have and need today. We live in a time in which we need new words, contemporary words, and archaic words, too, all at the same time. And we not only need to make them, we need to put them to creative and collaborative use.

I focus on the term "sharing" because it's the best place I know to begin, and I firmly believe we will not be able to move forward without it. But because some of the words we need weren't available to previous generations, this is a time in which we should also *thoughtfully* make our own on an as needed basis. Not so that we can attempt to win imaginary competitions, try to invent the coolest and most unique words, continue to overproduce and overconsume, or erase past contributions, but so that we can have words to strategically use and collaborate with. Given that the positions scholars take are not always as mutually exclusive as they seem, there are times when a dose of specificity in the words we use, along with a dose of patience, perhaps, might work like a dose of preventative medicine. We can push on promising ideas to make them stronger without cancelling, co-opting, or tearing them down. The Anthropocene is one of them.

"Shadowtime" may be another. The term comes from The Bureau of Linguistic Reality, a collaborative project that was established to create a new vocabulary for the Anthropocene. Of the dozen or so entries that have been suggested thus far, "Shadowtime" is among those gaining the most traction.[19] It's conceptualized as

> a parallel timescale that follows one around throughout day to day experience of regular time. Shadowtime manifests as a feeling of living in two distinctly different temporal scales simultaneously, or acute consciousness of the possibility that the near future will be drastically different than the present... While one may feel that Shadowtime follows them always, the sudden experience of the presence of Shadowtime amid day to day activities is often extremely disorienting.[20]

Living under the shadow of the Anthropocene can be, as the Bureau suggests in another entry, *pre*-traumatic. And, in a way, that is what being in the Anthropocene is like. It's like suddenly having a shadow attach to you that you can't escape, one that, in place of intrusive flashbacks, leads to disruptive flashforwards, instead. And, as I write this in real time, I notice that by coincidence, or by synchronicity, or by creepy algorithms, perhaps, Daniel Saint Black's song "Shadow"[21] has begun to stream online. We're living in the shadow of a new epoch: one that continues to claim us without consent, ignoring how much we'd rather be left alone.

Part of why it's difficult to respond to the Anthropocene, then, is that it's too big to see. As Timothy Morton writes, the scope of the Anthropocene is larger than we can comprehend, even as it's already here.[22] The enormity of the problem makes it easier to remain within a state of denial, a state of denial that we then choose to take refuge in. As a way of avoiding psychological distress and the feelings of complicity that go along with it, we participate in what Kari Norgaard describes as collective avoidance and socially organized denial. Instead of taking responsibility and confronting this challenge directly, we hide. As she writes in *Living in Denial*, we do this because we would rather not think about it. We would rather choose not to know.[23] We would prefer to close the door, get back in bed under the covers, and stay in our rooms, pretending as if nothing bad is happening outside.

But that won't do, not if we are to survive. We have to come to terms with what is happening in the world around us, and, in the process, we have to come to terms with ourselves.

Miss Anthropocene

Creative collaborations offer venues in which we can collectively come to terms. The album *Miss Anthropocene,* for instance, was fashioned to do just that. It was created by Claire Elise Boucher, a Canadian artist who has preferred to do professional work under the name Grimes (which is how I refer to her here). The album is worth attending to closely.

In promotional interviews prior to the album's 2020 release, Grimes described *Miss Anthropocene* as "a concept album about the anthropomorphic goddess of climate change," in which "each song will be a different embodiment of human extinction.'[24] In another interview around the same time, she gave a related, if slightly more specific response:

> 'It's a concept album, about anthropomorphizing climate change,' she says. Miss Anthropocene is 'like, this death god.' But also: 'It's fun. I want to make climate change fun. People don't care about it, because we're being guilted. I see the polar bear and want to kill myself. No one wants to look at it, you know? I want to make a reason to look at it. I want to make it beautiful.'[25]

As Grimes points out, the Anthropocene is depressing. It's easy to slide into the isolation of sadness, hopelessness, and despair when we're not able to effectuate instant change. And while I think the idea of a concept album about the Anthropocene is fascinating—especially one with an anti-hero—I also question how well the concepts of climate change and fun go together. For me, they don't. Although Grimes subsequently clarified her initial remarks, expressing that her aim was to raise awareness of, and engagement with, the issue of climate change,[26] her clarifications did not ameliorate concerns. They did, however, continue to generate a lot of attention.

The initial reviews of *Miss Anthropocene* have been mixed, which is unsurprising given the controversies that the album has seemed to invite. As one reviewer commented, for instance, "In this very specific political moment, rendering climate crisis as dystopian aesthetic is privileged and indulgent."[27] And that would be true, I think, *if* that's all it was, and if some of the sharpest political critiques were not already known to intentionally cut deeply to the core. The full impact of the album will not be immediate; there's a lot to unpack here, too, and futuristic predictions always need time to play out. So, given that this *is* a very specific political moment, and given that the Anthropocene did come about through actions involving privilege and indulgence, I am left with the questions of, Why this album? Why now?

Although I am still thinking and will be for quite some while, on balance, I would point to the review that describes *Miss Anthropocene* as "a dark record, at times almost indefensibly nihilistic, but at its best it recalls modern horror movies... [that] frighten us with a larger purpose in mind—to shock us into rethinking certain attitudes."[28] It seems important how, as another reviewer noted, the song "Violence" offers a compelling yet "disturbing analogy between an abusive relationship and humanity's sadistic/masochistic relationship with the Earth."[29] And I, for one, find that the details of the album come together well, even if others find it "chaotic."[30] For instance, toward the beginning of "Darkseid," Grimes observes that because we live so much in a digital world, we no longer bother to move our bodies in the real one; she circles back to this idea toward the end. Additionally, titles such as "Delete Forever" are memorable reminders of what is at stake.

Similar to other reviewers, I am curious as to why a particular song was omitted from the final version. "We Appreciate Power" is a song, or cynical anthem, perhaps, about submitting to a future controlled by AI.[31] It seems to have been meant as a provocative precursor to the album, and yet, it's not here. Maybe it has already done its work by signaling a broader question about what it means to be human in the face of AI, or maybe it's a question of whether, soon, we will even be human at all. The word "transhuman" does seem to be popping up more and more. Or, maybe the song "New Gods" offers insights into her thinking, as do interview comments in which she wonders if she is among the last of humans who will make art because AI will soon take this on.[32]

What a time we live in that she would wonder this out loud. It makes me consider whether she, and perhaps others, are trying to communicate several very difficult ideas through art—ideas with which, whether we avoid them or not, we will be forced to contend.

We should not commodify the end of the world in our outputs, and I hope this album ultimately isn't that. We produce and consume too much already, and unless we want to keep producing and consuming the end of the world, we must change how we go about both. As Grimes warns us in a satirical letter posted online before the album released, if we continue at the rate we are going and do not slow down, we will "burn twice as bright and half as long."[33]

And given what is transpiring, perhaps, just perhaps, as Grimes suggests in "Before the Fever," when we hear the sound of the end of the world, we should dance through the night.

Notes

1 Cannella, "Histories and Possibilities," 16.
2 Silverstein, "Prayer of the Selfish Child," 15.
3 Ulmer, "Photogenic Images," 121.
4 Salvo, *Reading Autoethnography*, 129.
5 *Webster's New International Dictionary*. "Collaborate," 524.
6 *The Compact Edition of the Oxford English Dictionary*, "Collaborate," 1464.
7 *The Compact Edition of the Oxford English Dictionary,* "Share," 2770.
8 *The Oxford English Dictionary Online*, "Share," para. 1, emphasis in original.
9 *Webster's New International Dictionary*, "Share," 2303.
10 Korsgaard, *Fellow Creatures*, 3.
11 Tuana, "Climate Apartheid," 3.
12 Ibid., 19.
13 Nancy, *Being Singular Plural*, 23.
14 Nancy, *Being Singular Plural*, 2.
15 Nancy, *The Inoperative Community*, 64.
16 Thompson, "It's Not Just the Great Lakes," para. 1.
17 Ibid., para. 2–3.
18 See also, Nordstrom, "Practices of Care."
19 See also Hyde et. al, "Shadowtime."
20 *The Bureau of Linguistic Reality*, "Shadowtime," 1–3.
21 In Black, "Shadow."
22 E.g., Morton, *Hyperobjects*.
23 Norgaard, *Living in Denial*, 7–8.
24 Grimes, qtd. in Bloom and Blais-Billie, "Grimes Announces New Album," para. 1–2.
25 Grimes, qtd. in Bradley, "The Life and Death of Grimes," para. 25.
26 Richards, "'Miss Anthropocene' Is Excellent," para 13.
27 Mistry, "Grimes," para. 8.
28 Hermes, "Review," para. 2.
29 Jackson and Bell, "Grimes's New Album," para. 11.
30 Lefevre, "Here's What Critics Are Saying," para. 1.
31 Jackson and Bell, "Grimes's New Album," para. 11; Mistry, "Grimes," para. 4.
32 Weisenstein, "Grime's Album," para. 9.
33 Grimes, "Letter," para. 6.

References

Black, Daniel Saint. "Shadow." On *Shadow* [CD]. 17 Jan. 2020. Daniel Saint Black / Tone Tree Music.

Bloom, Madison, and Braudie Blais-Billie. "Grimes Announces New Album Miss_Anthropocene." *Pitchfork*, 20 March 2019, https://pitchfork.com/news/grimes-announces-new-album-miss-anthropocene/.

Bradley, Ryan. "The Life and Death of Grimes." *WSJ Magazine*, 20 March 2019, www.wsj.com/articles/the-life-and-death-of-grimes-11553084548.

Cannella, Gaile. "Histories and Possibilities." In *Critical Qualitative Inquiry: Foundations and Futures*, edited by Gaile Cannella, Michelle Salazar Pérez, and Penny A. Pasque, Left Coast Press, 2015, pp. 7–30.

Collaborate. In: *The Compact Edition of the Oxford English Dictionary,* vol. 2, Oxford UP, 1971/1986, p. 1464.

——. In: *Webster's New International Dictionary,* 2nd edition, G. & C. Merriam Company, 1934, p. 524.

Grimes. "Letter." Instagram post, 10 Feb. 2020, www.instagram.com/p/B8YA2w_HMGz/?utm_source=ig_embed.

Hermes, Will. "Review: On 'Miss Anthropocene,' Grimes Crafts Pop Both Visceral And Cryptic." *National Public Radio*, 24 Feb. 2020. www.npr.org/2020/02/24/808839481/review-on-miss-anthropocene-grimes-crafts-pop-both-visceral-and-cryptic.

Hyde, Emily, Kate Marshall, John M. G. Plotz, Monika Gehlawat, Kevin Brazil, Melanie Micir, and Aaron D. Rosenberg. "Shadowtime." Session delivered at the annual conference of the Modern Language Association, Chicago, 5 Jan. 2019.

Jackson, Dan, and Sadie Bell. "Grimes's New Album Is a Thrilling Journey Through an Apocalyptic Future." *Thrillist,* 24 Feb. 2020, www.thrillist.com/entertainment/nation/grimes-miss-anthropocene-review.

Korsgaard, Christine Marion. *Fellow Creatures: Our Obligations to the Other Animals*. Oxford UP, 2018.

Lefevre, Jules. "Here's What Critics Are Saying About Grimes' 'Chaotic' New Album." *Junkee*, 24 Feb. 2020, https://junkee.com/grimes-miss-anthropocene/243428.

Morton, Timothy. *Hyperobjects: Philosophy and Ecology After the End of the World.* University of Minnesota Press, 2013.

Nancy, Jean-Luc. *Being Singular Plural*. 1996. Translated by Robert D. Richardson, Stanford UP, 2000.

——. *The Inoperative Community*. Translated by Peter Connor, Lisa Garbus, Michael Holland, and Simona Sawhney, University of Minnesota Press, 1991.

Nordstrom, Susan Naomi. "Practices of Care with the Anthropocene: Scenes from the 2019 Nebraska Flood." In Jesse Bazzul, Maria F. G. Wallace, and Marc Higgins, editors, *Science x Education x Anthropocene*. Palgrave MacMillan, in progress.

Norgaard, Kari Marie. *Living in Denial: Climate Change, Emotions, and Everyday Life*. MIT Press, 2011.

Richards, Jared. "'Miss Anthropocene' Is Excellent, If You Ignore Everything Grimes Has Said About It." *Junkee Music*, 25 Feb. 2020, https://junkee.com/miss-anthropocene-grimes-review/243335.

Salvo, James. *Reading Autoethnography: Reflections on Justice and Love*. Routledge, 2020.

Shadowtime. In *The Bureau of Linguistic Reality*, 2015, https://bureauo flinguisticalreality.com/portfolio/shadowtime/.

Share. In: *The Compact Edition of the Oxford English Dictionary,* vol. 2. Oxford UP, 1971/1986, p. 2770.

——. In: *The Oxford English Dictionary Online.* Oxford UP, 2006/2015, n.p.

——. In: *Webster's New International Dictionary,* 2nd edition. G. & C. Merriam Company, 1934, p. 2303.

Silverstein, Shel. "Prayer of the Selfish Child." In *A Light in the Attic,* HarperCollins Children's Books, 1981, p. 15.

Thompson, Carol. "It's Not Just the Great Lakes. Flooding Threatens Inland Michigan, Too." *Lansing State Journal,* 23 Feb. 2020, www.lansingstatejournal. com/story/news/2020/02/24/experts-warn-spring-flooding-throughout-michigan-2020/4808160002/.

Tuana, Nancy. "Climate Apartheid: The Forgetting of Race in the Anthropocene." *Critical Philosophy of Race,* vol. 7, no. 1, 2019, pp. 1–31.

Ulmer, Jasmine Brooke. "Photogenic Images: Producing Everyday Gestures of Possibility." *The Reasons and Emotions of Images,* a dossier in *RBSE Revista Brasileira De Sociologia Da Emoção,* vol. 16, no. 47, 2017, pp. 117–133.

Weisenstein, Kara. "Grimes's Album 'Miss Anthropocene' is a Masterful Meditation on Humanity's Demise." *Mic,* 25, Feb. 2020, www.mic.com/ p/grimess-album-miss-anthropocene-is-a-masterful-meditation-on-humanitys-demise-22413855.

3   When the sun kisses the moon

A photographic interlude

Figure 3.1 Arabesque 1, 2018, Groningen, the Netherlands.

Figure 3.2 Arabesque 2, 2018, Groningen, the Netherlands.

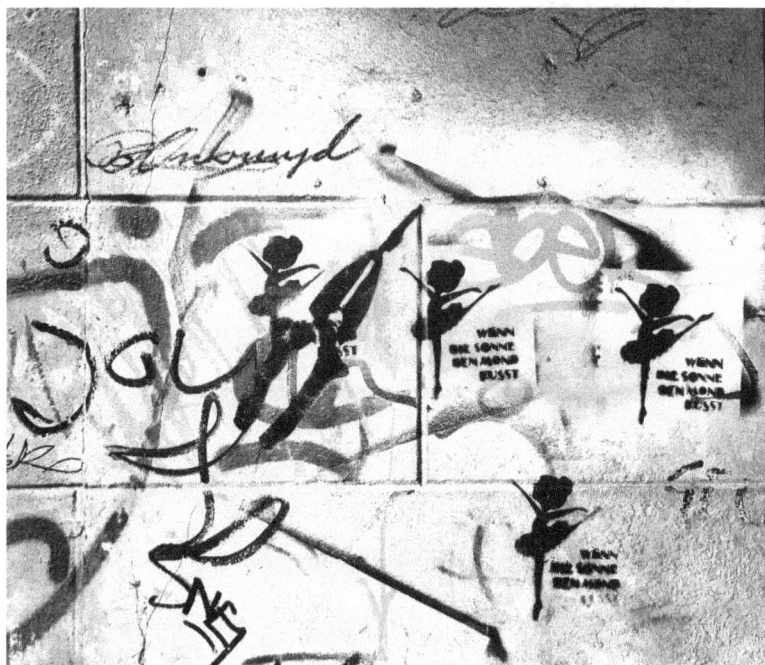

Figure 3.3 Arabesque 3, 2018, Groningen, the Netherlands.

Figure 3.4 Arabesque 4, 2018, Groningen, the Netherlands.

4   Choreographing through chaos

As Maxine Greene observes, "There are some who suggest that, of all the arts, dance confronts most directly the question of what it means to be human."[1] This is why I turn to dance: given that we are living in a time in which the future of humanity is uncertain due to climate change, the possibility of extinction, and the indeterminacies of AI, this question worth revisiting. What *does* it mean to be human, not only for ourselves, but also in relation to one another? Further, how can dance bring these ideas into scholarly writing? How is dance a way to share?

Dance is a force—one with the capacity to reshape society, culture, and ourselves. Choreographers craft powerful responses to contemporary issues through movement, dancers make those and other movements come alive, and both, alongside audiences, communicate not only who we are, but—for better or worse—who we might become. Dance draws from deeply held experiences and emotions to offer paths from our present realities toward more hopeful futures. At its best, dance is movement, sparks movement, moves bodies and minds. Dance compels us toward others in a more relational world.

To begin, dance is potentially world-changing, but only if it accomplishes certain things. Dance develops individuals *and* collectives. And, at the same time that it teaches us to be ourselves, it also teaches us how to contribute to, innovate from, and situate our work within larger traditions. This is important because, in order to change the world, we need to be our own selves *and* work with others to retain the best of what we have already learned. When we open up traditions by adding to them, we expand our repertoires as dancers and our capacities as human beings. In other words, when we do these things, we share.

Revolutions are such that they don't throw everything out and start from scratch, just like they don't stay mired in how things have always been done; revolutions call for a little pinch of both. Growing up as a dancer, I was familiar with these understandings. It was only later in life that I came to know them as a researcher, too—that I learned how two separate practices could apply the same techniques to achieve different effects. When we take the lessons dance already knows and apply them to research, we increase the possibility of our creative and academic work being a force for change.

In wanting inquiry to move with the power of dance, I often wonder how dance-infused writing might realize its potential as an innovative approach to inquiry—one in which dance scholars, practitioners, and educators might write with, from, through, and about dance. One in which writing comes from a place of movement that challenges us to reach beyond what we thought we were capable of in all we do. To leave everything on the dance floor at the end of a performance, only to return the next day and do it all again as if for the first time. Not to compete or prove anything to anyone else, but to contribute. To collaborate. To share. To find what we already have inside us as a way to push past the noise, get to our best selves, and lead meaningful lives. And to explore the ingredients in dance and inquiry that, together, can reshape the world.

Writing revolutions

The urgent troubles of our times demand nothing less. As choreographers like Hofesh Shechter know well, these are times that call for the same revolutionary energies we give to dance. This is why the Hofesh Schechter Company starts from the vision that dance has the potential to change lives and make the world a better place. This entails, however, much more than expert application of rote technical movements. In Shechter's company, this begins with dancers being themselves. For it is when dancers move from the core of who they are that they

> cut through layers of artifice to reveal things for what they really are, the raw truth, biting life at its core... [and] make people aware, awake, and in turn understand they hold the power to change.[2]

As he continues, "We dance to know what it feels like, not just to live, but to be alive."[3]

Some dance, therefore, to be alive. Others write to connect, heal, and tap into the same energies. Dancing and writing—when taken separately and together—encourage movement when life would otherwise hold us still; both offer paths through this chaotic, spinning world. A world which, like the dancers within it, continues to rotate, revolve, and return.

Rotational moves are an important aspect of dance as a force for social change, for even when we turn in place, we can generate revolutionary movements from where we already are. And when we write from who we already are, albeit in ways that may seem too small to be meaningful at first, we can return to what's important and patch together collective movements in dance research. But how, especially when it is so easy to get lost within the larger scholarly apparatus? I suggest we return to ourselves by taking cues from dance choreography. That we learn to write through life's chaos along threads of continuity that we find and create. And that we connect beyond our usual circles of influence to emphasize that the point of inquiry isn't to achieve individual success, but to collectively interpret and change the world. One motion, one note, one rotation at a time.

Writing dance

Dance is based in movement and writing is based in words. Because it is challenging to capture the spirit of embodied movements in writing, this can present a conundrum of sorts for dance scholars. Namely, dance movements draw from an entirely separate language. The language of dance is based upon rhythm, energy, posture, sequence, and presence; it is a language where gestures carry meaning, and where sense is located in the body but escapes from it at the same time. Dance is a language that dancers share.[4]

There are inherent tensions, then, between writing and movement. Tensions that, though not insurmountable, do produce challenges that should be approached with care in scholarship that invokes dance. One way to address these obstacles is to develop a thoughtful, committed practice in both dance and research. This includes attending to the concepts being put into use. Take, for example, choreography. Choreography is a term specific to dance: it originated from the Greek for dance (*khoreios* or *khoros*) and it has pertained to dance since. Yet, everyone starts somewhere, and the possibilities of dance extend an open invitation to those with the desire to learn. What is wonderful is that it is never too late to begin. Dance encourages us all to move toward what we did not know what we were yet capable of, to learn skills and techniques, and to stretch but not hyperextend. From recreation to rehabilitation, dance is an inclusive practice that offers opportunities to belong. It does this by extending across disability, age, refugee status, gender, sexuality, citizenship, language, race, ethnicity, faith, and other aspects of identity. And whether in formal or informal capacities, dance invites bodies to move so that thoughts might move, too.

Dance inspires writing to do the same—to shift bodies, minds, and spirits by embodying movement as a force for political, social, and cultural change. A thoughtful dance practice encourages us to become better writers, just as it insists that we continue to grow and develop as dancers, choreographers, and everyday people. In these ways, dance offers something to hold onto in moments when the world shakes us to our core, generating the sparks we need to begin moving again. Dance allows us to connect with something much larger than ourselves, whether that be in reciprocity with the planet, in connection with humanity, or, for some, perhaps something more spiritual. Dance takes up collective ideals to depart from individualism, bring us together, locate what is actually meaningful, and, when those seem to have been lost, suggest a path for return. When taken in tandem, dance and writing are a formidable combination: in facilitating productive movements, they show us how we do not have to start all over again in order to start at all. They point to where we might find safety in troubled times, how we might respond, and who we might become. They remind us not only of what revolution is, but how we might go back to the importance of what we do. Both dance and writing bring us to truth.

Dancing change

Dance shows us possibilities that have been in front of us. In mirroring extant realities, dance shows us not only who we are, but how we might become who we aspire to be. Communicated in choreography and expressed through performance, dance—in being repeated again and again—can have a profound influence upon dancers and audiences alike: dance depicts what we otherwise would not see. As Pirkko Markula writes, "an artistic work makes what is currently imperceptible perceptible in the social world."[5] *This* is the force of dance.

Because dance differs from other forms of art, it uniquely enables us to facilitate change. Unlike other art genres, dance is based in movement, requires active bodies, combines media, and engages audiences differently in participation and interpretation. Dance can also seem less representational to us than other art forms. It does not include the ability to create true-to-life images, objects, or speech. Paintings, photographs, videos, sculptures, installations, textiles, scripts, prose, and myriad other media do that instead, often within fixed two- and three-dimensional representations. Further, dance helps us shift away from stories that are conveyed through words and visual images—from the everyday communications with which we are familiar, whether in artistic or objective form. It's in this shift that dance allows us to express our innermost selves in gestures and movements, breaking through the confines of our daily habits and routines.

Dance comments on the lives we lead and how we live them, both as individual and collective members of humanity. This is important, for dance is one of the only arts that currently requires the visible presence of live human bodies. Even when artists depict humans in paintings, photographs, or sculptures, for instance, we can still experience that piece of artwork alone; the original subjects and creators need not be there. Moreover, we watch theatrical productions with puppets, television shows involving clay animations or cartoons, and films that generate characters from digital technologies. Music is also increasingly digitally made. Yet, dance remains distinctive in that it is the only one to need human bodies. Dance cannot exist without dancers in this reality as we know it, for dance exists in the moment. It can be filmed and replayed later, to be sure, but in the initial moment, at least, dancers must be present to perform. There is an interplay in performances, then, in which dancers express themselves through movements that are conveyed to, received by, and interpreted by live audiences. While dancers communicate with audiences and audiences communicate with dancers, both experience the tension between individual and collective consciousness.

It is precisely this tension between individuals and society that drives Shechter's choreographic practice. At the age of eighteen, Shechter was not only studying at the Jerusalem Academy of Dance and Music, he was also fulfilling compulsory military service obligations. Being engaged in conflict sparked many questions for Shechter, especially with regard to the agency of individuals. He explains,

> As humans, we want to think of ourselves as free and unique, yet we still allow ourselves to become cogs in a machine. I couldn't understand how it happens. Is there anyone driving this huge truck we are all sitting in? What comes first, the individual or the mass?[6]

Though it has been two decades since he completed military service, such wonderings have continued to thread throughout his work, as have attempts to engage and better humanity through dance. He has since used choreography to make sense of the world and help others do the same. Patching together emotionally charged fragments of the human experience to envision alternative ways of moving and living. Engaging dance to catalyse social and cultural change. And, in the process, challenging our bodies, minds, spirits, and relationships with each other and ourselves. For Shechter, this is purposeful.

Choreographing through (the) chaos

The world can be chaotic. Though no one is immune from the chaos that affects us all, too often, we experience the confusions, disruptions, and upheavals of daily life alone. The titles of many of Shechter's choreographic productions bear this out: *Fragments*. *Uprising*. *Survivor*. *Political Mother*. *The Art of Not Looking Back*. And *In Your Rooms*, the work I'll briefly describe here.

In Your Rooms has been one of Shechter's most important contributions to date. Debuting in 2007 and successively expanding in size and scope, the piece was crafted for three different performance spaces in London. It is a contemporary masterpiece that explores the collective impulses of humanity and the efforts of individuals to escape from worldwide cycles of violence and oppression that not only unfold publicly in the streets, but also in the isolation of our homes. Vitality courses throughout the piece, which addresses what it means and how it feels to be alive.

The production begins in simple fashion. Core phrases of music and movements provide a quiet backdrop for an opening monologue from Shechter. In it, he describes "the cosmos as a complex thing, full of endless, rather chaotic elements and details that float in endless space, something one would say is random in ways."[7] As *In Your Rooms* continues, it goes on to work within this chaos, showing how— when thought together—our lives might be more similarly patterned than they initially appear. From upheaval to mass conflict to intimate partner violence, Shechter hints at all-too-common themes as he puts the momentums of humanity on display, illustrating how easily it can be for individuals to be absorbed into the mass and become cogs in a directionless machine. Forged from chaos, the piece helps make sense of the seemingly random, chaotic, uncontrollable elements in our lives. Not to create further disruptions, but to rearrange and respond to chaos through both dance and music.

Notably, Shechter—who once drummed for a band called the Human Beings—co-composed the musical score and was among the original percussionists. It is unusual to maintain an artistic practice involving both dance and music: dance choreographers rarely compose music. Yet, the combination here is powerful, as each element breathes life into the other. This is particularly noticeable mid-performance when the small group of live musicians is revealed—hidden from the audience, they have been playing in a room concealed above the dancers at the back of the stage. The tempo changes. Although *In Your Rooms* has unfolded slowly, calmly adding layers of music and dance onto one another, it now begins to escalate alongside increasingly urgent drumbeats. The piece culminates in an explosive, uncontainable crescendo as dancers move with the full passions of the human spirit. They move against the negative undercurrents of humanity, showing how much effort, energy, and counter momentum is needed for meaningful change to occur. To live differently. To be free. To find release.

Our bodies can hold onto physical and emotional events long after the initial moments in which they occurred came to pass. These are the sorts of embodied memories to which Shechter and many other choreographers (and composers) return. In particular, it is not uncommon for choreographers to describe how dance releases the residual emotions that bodies retain. This is why choreographers can go back and forth between phrases of movement and phrases of music— to see what might be felt and expressed and liberated through music. Shechter shares that he does this through chaos: it is through choreography that he draws from, productively uses, and responds to the chaos that surrounds. Given that emotions play a central role in his work, it is perhaps unsurprising that *In Your Rooms* seems to counter chaos through an emotional array that includes pain, frustration, perseverance, isolation, grief, anxiety, hope, fear, and others. As performers dance these emotions throughout the performance, audiences are left to consider how embodied memories can hold us back from connecting with one another—can confine us as emotional prisoners when we isolate ourselves in our own rooms. There are times when we must move our bodies to counter the unrest in our souls, when we must dance to feel free.[8]

Choreography, therefore, listens to our bodies and responds through movement. It begins with what bodies already know, sense, remember, and feel. It communicates, connects, and awakens. And it moves through chaos in ways that are not only affective, but in ways that can be visceral, as well, as jazz drummer Milford Graves explains. But first, we have to listen to our bodies to find the beat.

Chaos heartbeats

Graves' philosophy of drumming involves finding and moving to your own heartbeat. In observing that heart rates change and vary as part of normal daily life, he notes that our bodies expect these changes and variations. Our bodies expect to move at different speeds at different times. This is why Graves takes heart rate variability as a marker of being alive, both in a literal and figurative sense. From his perspective, it would be alarming if hearts moved like metronomes, perfectly synchronized to one (and only one) rhythm: we are neither robots nor people marching through life with exact military precision. We are human beings and, as such, we should attune with our surroundings. Graves remarks,

> If you felt your pulse rate at your wrist or any other place other than listening to your heart... they should be different. That's a healthy heartbeat. They can call that the chaos heartbeat. They can call that heart rate variability, that means the rate constantly varies. And in order to do that all people have to do is feel their pulse and all of a sudden if they count they'll notice that they're counting slow at one point and then they're counting a little faster. That's great. But if you count like a metronome and everything... just like the second-hand, that is extremely dangerous. That means your body is not responding. It must *respond*.[9]

It would be unwise to simply let life unfold as if nothing is at stake, sitting by as if we really are just cogs in a machine. What we must do instead, Graves insists, is respond. We must allow our bodies to acknowledge, react to, engage, and work from the chaos. Outlets such as drumming offer one way. Or, as in Shechter's case, the pairing of drumming and dance offers another.

Drumming is similar to dance. Drumbeats sound out the pulses—rhythms—heartbeats of humanity, the desires to live, the frustrations of living, the variable cadences of life. Through embodied, practiced, and performative movements, drummers link with others in their immediate vicinity; in so doing, they also relate within an interconnected world.[10] These are all significant aspects of *In Your Rooms*, especially with respect to how—after the musicians are brought into view—there is a moment in which the drummers and dancers briefly unite.

At one point in the performance, the dancers line up across the back of the stage and—in rapid succession to the beat of the drums—repeatedly pound their hands in the air as if beating on an invisible wall, trying to break free from the rooms that confine us (or, rather, from the rooms that we continue to confine ourselves in). Together, the musicians and dancers show us how, when faced with hardships, we can end up withdrawing into ourselves. Hiding. Retreating. Feeling separate and alone. In this moment, for me, at least, the drums seem to juxtapose the urgent punctuations of a local here and now against the sweeping currents of destructive global forces. Meanwhile, the staccato drumbeats seem to interrupt the longer, flowing, unifying notes of the stringed instruments, calling to mind the dangers of gunfire, rebellion, domestic violence, and the urge to escape it all. In these ways and potentially others, the choreography of *In Your Rooms* challenges us to reconsider the different ways we are isolated from the world, particularly when it comes to how humans sow the seeds of chaos for themselves and other human beings.

Amidst widespread and systemic turmoil, it is indeed difficult to know what to do next. One impulse can be to counter chaos with more chaos. I would argue, though, that creating chaos mostly serves as a temporary distraction—and that those who do so are engaging in an attempt to hide from others as they ultimately attempt to hide from themselves. Yet, *In Your Rooms* shows us that isolation is neither desirable nor fully doable in a global world. We cannot keep hiding, whether through active diversions or passive withdrawals. All too often, instigating chaos is designed to seek attention rather than promote meaningful, sustainable change; in instances when individual desires overshadow collective needs, chaos distracts from far more urgent priorities.

We cannot continue to stay in our rooms, for instance, and be exempt from the ways we are damaging the planet through warming temperatures, rising seas, and so on. Many of those rooms will only continue to get hotter, wetter, and less livable with time. This is a different, though not unrelated, sort of chaos. The chaos to which Shechter responds primarily involves what humans do to other humans, and he harnesses that chaos to produce something that counters the harmful effects thereof. In contrast, this second type of chaos is more-than-human. Stemming from accelerated climate changes and ecological collapse, the chaos of the Anthropocene spreads through what Anna Tsing describes as "detonators" that are embedded within our global infrastructures; Tsing makes sense of chaos by thinking about movement within and across systems.[11] Even though Shechter and Tsing attend to different concerns in different disciplines, both ground their responses in movement. And in this present moment—one marked by the violence that humans inflict not only on each other, but upon all life on this planet—I imagine both might agree. We don't need anarchy: we need revolution.

Revolutionary movements

Revolutions are a key form of movement in dance. Turning is part of what dancers do, and there are many ways to turn. For dancers, revolutions are a routine part of everyday life. As a former dancer, this is how I came to approach revolution through dance; this is also how this chapter, this book, and related articles came to be. One of the last things I wrote before conceptualizing this book was the commentary, "*Pivots* and *Pirouettes*: Carefully Turning Traditions." In it, I had added a coda—a coda meant to create a thread of continuity that I could return to here. I wrote,

> When dancers turn through *pivots* and *pirouettes*, they are revolving. They are spinning, rotating, turning, and returning. They are reorienting to the world while moving in place, showing that revolutions can happen from within us—from within our cores— from where we already are. This is another way to think through the concept of revolution.[12]

As I was writing the last words of that piece, I knew that I would want to return to the ways in which dance shows us how the capacity for revolution is already within us.

I appreciate how dance reminds us that we can return to what we know is meaningful and to the strengths we already have. We do not have to become someone else or go someplace else to make a difference in the world. We can dance as ourselves, for choreography teaches us to move from who, where, when, why, and how we are. Not just individually, but collectively—existing in reciprocity with those around us, recognizing all that we and those around us have to offer. In these ways, dance encourages us to do our best thinking, together, as we acknowledge what humanity does to itself and to the other species with which we share the world. Dance helps us move through the darkness, and the strengths of dance are worth remembering indeed.

Continuity is one such strength. As a continuously evolving form of art, dance innovates through continuity: choreographers shift, adapt, and expand their repertoires in relation to the rich pasts, presents, and futures of dance. In other words, choreographers do not operate in a vacuum when they craft a fresh performance. It is well-understood that dance techniques and traditions build collectively over time, and that dancers and choreographers will contribute to the body of work that already exists. Innovations, of course, are welcomed, for innovations are a key tradition within dance. This allows movements, positions, and choreographies to be passed down from one generation of dancers to the next over time.

Continuities not only create a sense of community, but a place to return. This isn't an actual location, unless you're in my former ballet studio where the word 'spot' had been painted in large, black, letters across the stage right wall of the practice room for young dancers. Spotting is a technique that allows dancers to execute multiple turns. To spot, dancers their fix their eyes on a particular point and keep their head stationary for as long as possible; as the rest of their body turns, their head whips back around to that same position, eyes reorienting to the designated point, ideally over and over again. Whether we were practicing *pirouettes* in place or spinning in a straight line from one side of the room to the other through *chaîné* turns, we held our attention at that spot on the wall. Spotting fostered balance and internal momentum as it prevented dizziness—spotting kept us from stumbling, falling down, and spinning out of control. As we grew older and graduated into a larger studio, we were subsequently trained to create a point of focus wherever we were at. To look for something that might be there, or, if necessary, to imagine something ourselves. This helped us to not get lost in revolutions. It also taught us that we could always locate a place of return.

This is important, because revolution involves return. Revolt does, as well.

Both come from the Latin term *volvere*, which means to roll or to turn. The addition of the prefix *re-* to *volvere*, then, entails rolling or turning again. This is not, however, how we have generally come to approach these terms in the last 200 years. For Julia Kristeva, this is a mistake:

> What has been taken for revolt or revolution for two centuries, particularly in politics and its attendant ideologies, has more often been this abandonment of retrospective questioning in favor of a rejection, pure and simple, of the old, destined to be replaced by new dogmas.[13]

Kristeva argues that the terms revolution and revolt departed from their own etymology after the French Revolution, when they were misunderstood as upheaval or overthrowal. Since then, she writes, these terms have carried not only a sense of romantic mysticism, but nihilism. This can be dangerous, for nihilism remains fixed in the celebration of two extremes: "rejection of the old or in the unquestioned positivity of the new."[14] We should do more, she suggests, than pursue newness for the sake of novelty, as being novel is not the same thing as being important. In this vein, revolt and revolution offer useful concepts when we reach impasses in thinking; rather than requiring us to reject everything that has come before—through acts of return—they invite us to constructively and productively shift into what comes next.

Dance choreography provides an example of how this can be done. But before exploring how, it is perhaps useful to recognize that we live in a highly complex world. Of the many smart and insightful thinkers throughout human history, there are few who would claim to have all the answers alone. And given the urgent troubles of the world (including the future of humanity and other species on this planet), it is necessary that we all think our best thoughts, together. This does not, of course, mean adhering only to what has been done before. Nor does it mean erasing or rejecting all traditions in order to supplant the old with something that is being presented as new—very little, after all, is truly new. There is balance to be had. In embracing this approach, Shechter fosters equilibrium through relationality. He aligns choreographic movements to what he knows, remembers, feels, is inspired by, and has learned from others. And while "that takes away any sense of uniqueness—it does give a strong sense of connection though, of linking things."[15] Linking via connection offers another form of revolution and return, one which can be radical.

Making connections is a necessary ingredient in social and cultural revolutions. Without them, change does not occur and we are instead left with isolated and unrelated incidents that quickly come and go, fade from memory, and get subsumed in the chaos. This is how dance helps us approach revolution: just as choreographers link repeatable dance movements together, activists link repeatable social justice movements together to generate and sustain change over time. In other words, revolution, like choreography, operates from a series of movements that can be repeated in other moments and places. The civil rights movement is one example. Across the U.S. during the 1950s and 1960s, revolution was achieved through many strategic repetitions: sit-ins, marches, walks, Freedom Rides, boycotts, court challenges, legislation, art, and others. The civil rights movement was a concerted and collective effort, one whose anthem became "Dancing in the Streets," a song recorded on a Motown label by Martha and the Vandellas in 1964 Detroit. Yet, its lyrics were not aimed at inspiring a single city or even a single country: it became a powerful anthem because its relevance could be linked across the world.

Dance, then, offers a model for inspiring widespread social and cultural change. Choreography makes movements repeatable, which, in turn, shows how transformative actions can also be repeated. This is significant, because revolutions are rarely, if at all, improvised. Revolutions are the work of careful (albeit sometimes invisible) planning. Revolutions happen one movement at a time, rippling outward in different directions as small, repeatable, planned movements begin to coalesce. But repeatable does not mean purely replicable, as movements inevitably shift with each iteration; Deleuze reminds us that repetitions produce differences, creating important variations over time.[16] And though variations unfold differently—such as in the images of the dancers rotating with the text "when the sun kisses the moon"—variations can be different without having to be chaotic. Revolution and anarchy are indeed two different things, and revolutions need not always be dramatic. Revolutions can result from even the smallest shifts in practice.

Choreographic returns

Notably, revolutions do not exclude generative change. The relationship between classical ballet and contemporary dance is a good example of this, as it has come to be marked by reciprocity and appreciation. Just as ballet has created openings for contemporary dance over the last century, contemporary dance, in turn, has influenced certain approaches to ballet. Techniques from one oftentimes carry over into the styles, movements, positions, and ways of thinking of the other. Some of the most important innovations have come from choreographers revisiting the assumptions of movement, wondering why we move in the ways we do. Many of their innovations appear intuitive today.

For example, Martha Graham's approach to choreographic technique may have revolutionized 20th-century dance, but she accomplished this by putting very simple insights into use. One of the simplest had to do with the floor. Graham would lean, fall, spiral downward, and otherwise move in relation to the floor. This may not be unusual now, but prior to Graham's popularization of this technique (and Isadora Duncan's previous use thereof), gravity was a force to be opposed—not utilized—in dance. Ballerinas were supposed to move as if defying gravity: lightly, delicately, effortlessly, unnaturally. The floor was no place for ballerinas. Graham, then, did not only add floorwork to dance; she offered another spatial dimension in which dancers could move. A second insight from Graham involved finding a more natural position for dancers' legs and feet. Rather than the traditional "turnout" position, in which ballet dancers rotate their feet, legs, and hips outward, Graham established "parallel position." This was radical. Whereas many dancers once sought to create a single 180-degree line with both feet joined at the heels and splayed sideways (and still do), Graham proposed that feet might also be positioned facing forward, hip-distance apart, making two parallel lines. This relates to a third insight from Graham, who thought that toes needn't always be pointed. In summarizing her unconventional vision for movement, Reynolds writes, "Falls replaced leaps, and turn-out gave way to parallel legs and taut, flexed feet."[17]

Because they have been so fully absorbed into contemporary dance practice, none of these insights seem particularly profound today. In fact, suggestions to "use the floor," "put your feet in parallel," or "flex your toes" would be seen as rather mundane (as would Lester Horton's recommendations for engaging the whole body in dance). But there was a time not so long ago when each of these would have been unthinkable. What Graham teaches us, then, is that simple shifts can lead to large-scale revolutions. It can be a matter of sifting through the chaos to find where they might be located.

As Shechter might suggest, insightful shifts often hide in plain sight. There is a moment in *In Your Rooms*, for instance, when a dancer walks to the front of the stage. As he breaks the fourth wall to make direct contact with the audience, he holds up a small sign. He displays a message on the front before flipping it over to reveal another message that has been written on the back. It reads:

Don't follow leaders
Follow me

This is a message that certainly has the potential for tongue-in-cheek interpretations. As in, "Don't follow [those] leaders. Follow me [this leader]." Further, who are leaders, anyway? Politicians? Public figures? Trend-makers, tastemakers, and/or influencers? It's a moment of levity that gets laughs from the audience, but it also conveys a deeper meaning given the context of the production. A hint can found in the change in lighting. As the "Follow me" sign is displayed, the house lights are raised so that the audience can see itself. What Shechter is insinuating, therefore, is that we should choose to think and act for ourselves. We shouldn't just follow "them" because it is what "they" want us or expect us to do; we should actively participate in a collective "us" that begins with "me." We should respond to the world instead of being absorbed into its mass, for we can be much more than cogs in the machine. But to do so, we must be careful. We should not, for example, follow leaders without ideas; we must instead become willing and able to make a distinction between empty rhetoric and substance. We must also be willing to follow ourselves.

We must work collectively as our own selves, working in continuity with the best of what already has been done, avoiding conformity along the way. Though Martha Graham broke from centuries of traditions to create new ones within contemporary dance, like Alvin Ailey, she also continued to choreograph ballets. The most influential choreographers in dance history engage multiple traditions to expand the boundaries of dance: their work is radical and recognizable at the same time. This has allowed choreographers to leverage dance as a social force, for even audience members who are less familiar with dance have been able to appreciate the power of Ailey's *Revelations*. In describing the rich legacy of his signature work, Ailey's dance company writes that *Revelations*

> fervently explores the places of deepest grief and holiest joy in the soul… transcending barriers of faith and nationality, and appealing to universal emotions, making it the most widely-seen modern dance work in the world.[18]

Inspired by Ailey's embodied memories of being raised in rural segregation, the pieces are set to a moving score of traditional spirituals, gospel, and blues.[19] Although *Revelations* has been performed continuously across the world since it debuted in 1960, four years before the passage of the Civil Rights Act, it remains just as relevant today.

The depths of truth in a work contribute to its staying power, as *Revelations* and *In Your Rooms* both illustrate. Each brings to life what their respective choreographers came to know, feel, find, and share. Each were choreographed by artists who not only moved as themselves, but choreographed from their souls.

Writing revelations

To change the world, we must learn to move forward as ourselves. Though this is a big task, writing, inquiring, and dancing as ourselves are not as impossible as they might seem.

However much dancers might sometimes aim for the contrary, their individual movements differ, even when attempting to repeat the same choreographies and styles. Such variations can be thought of as movement signatures. In other words, even when dancers attempt to exactly repeat movements, individual differences always materialize. It happens naturally as dancers' previous training influences, choreographic memories, and personal experiences blend into a unique style that grows and develops over time. As such, Jenni Roche advises dance teachers to reconsider their approach to pedagogy. Instead of "train[ing] dancers to be a neutral palette in order to embody any or all styles,"[20] she suggests that instructors take the lead of choreographers who help dancers cultivate signature moving identities, thereby helping dancers to move as themselves.

Shechter creates choreography in relation to dancers, as does Mathilde Monnier. When crafting group performances, both leave room for dancers to express the same movements in different ways. Their dancers move together as part of a larger collective while still retaining elements of individuality: one isn't sacrificed on behalf of the other. Their impulse goes against the tendency to squish dancers into conforming to a particular choreographic style or vision—one which treats dancers not as people who are dancing, but as malleable, interchangeable units that serve at the pleasure of choreographers and artistic directors in order to animate the visions of others. Notably, Monnier and Shechter take a different approach.

In many fields, authors have room to develop signature moving identities in writing, too. From performance autoethnography to creative analytic practices in ethnography to narratives and poetic inquiries and more, qualitative inquiry offers an open invitation for writers to write as themselves. Yet, this is easier said than done. Though there are recognizable stylistic conventions in any discourse community and there is bound to be a certain degree of overlap, there is also a difference between writing within a particular genre and emulating the style of a specific author. Trying to legitimize one's work by sounding like another scholar misses the mark, especially within practices that have the desire to be artistic, creative, new, and/or different. Nothing new or different comes from endeavours to be someone else, and we are being unkind to ourselves when we try. We must be willing to give ourselves the gifts of patience and understanding when we write. It takes time to find ourselves as writers, as the question of how to write is separate from how to write as oneself. We have to know who we are to know what we can contribute, and writing is an important part of that developmental process. Like dancers who develop signature moving identities over the course of their careers, strong writers do the same.

And this, perhaps, is what's most appealing within calls to be new and different: the opportunity to think and write as ourselves. To not be forced into conforming to the unwanted, unwelcome constraints imposed on us by others in the name of convention. To neither be compelled to perform in service to someone else's vision nor pressured into writing as someone we are not. To instead find spaces in which we can explore creative impulses and artistic truths, spaces in which we can share the most vulnerable and vibrant parts of ourselves. For it is when we find the ability to dance and write as ourselves that we can do something that is new and different, as we are new and different just in being ourselves.

Being ourselves, though, is not the same thing as going at it alone. If we seclude ourselves in the aim of purely being ourselves, then we cannot be in conversation or community with others. Rather, that is when we can become isolated in our rooms—alienated from outside influences, quarantined from one another, unable to contribute to the world in spite of—and in response to—the chaos that surrounds. To write about dance with the power of dance in research, we need options beyond being a cog in the machine and unplugging from the machine entirely. Isolationism is a risk. When we separate from nearby scholars and discourse communities, we can overlook important contributions from the smart, insightful thinkers who came before us and who think alongside us now. It is easy to repeat the mistakes of the past and duplicate what has already been done in the rush past practice and technique, for it is impossible to determine what is truly new and different when we are unaware of what already exists. Moreover, we cannot effectively challenge troublesome conventions without absorbing the inner workings of a particular craft. As individuals, we and we alone cannot solve the complex challenges threatening humanity and all other life on this planet today. It will take collaborating together, and we should not overlook what others have already shared.

Being ourselves is also not the primary objective in research. Our aim involves understanding the world so that we can make positive contributions to it. We do this not by withdrawing from our dynamic, constantly changing, chaotic world, but by directly engaging with the most pressing problems of these troubled times. In other words, the end goal is not to develop a writing style so that it (or we) might be noticed, but so that it might do some good on the damaged planet we share. If we are to do anything other than further accelerate the effects of the Anthropocene, we must choose to generatively interact and communicate with those around us. Revolution is a community matter. Whether in dance or research or life, then, we must find ways of not only being our own selves, but being our *best* selves in relation to one another. We must dance in the streets—in community—in reciprocity—with hope—with others. If we all elected to unplug and do just that, the revolution would be invincible indeed.

As dancers, we are taught to practice different movements together, developing aspects of ourselves while also contributing to the greater whole. As inquirers, we can do the same: we can ask questions regarding what it means to be human, how dance brings us together in a shared and collaborative practice, and how dance manifests some of the simplest human truths.

Notes

1 Greene, *Releasing the Imagination*, 131.
2 Hofesh Schechter Company, "Our Story," para. 7.
3 Ibid., para. 2.
4 Monnier and Nancy, "Alliterations," 600.

5 Markula, "Body-Movement-Change," 357.
6 Schechter, qtd. in Mackrell, "Interview," para. 5.
7 "In Your Rooms," chor. Schechter, performance.
8 Andrade and Gutierrez-Perez, "Bailando Con las Sombras," 503.
9 Graves, qtd. in *Milford Graves Full Mantis*, video.
10 Pedri-Spade, "The Drum is Your Document," 385.
11 Tsing, "The More-Than-Human Anthropocene" lecture.
12 Ulmer, "Pivots and Pirouettes," 457, emphasis in original.
13 Kristeva, *Intimate Revolt*, 6.
14 Ibid., 6.
15 Shechter, qtd. in Moelwyn-Hughes et. al, *Barbarians*, 7.
16 E.g., Deleuze, *Difference and Repetition*.
17 Reynolds, "A Technique for Power," 18.
18 Alvin Ailey American Dance Theater, "Revelations," para. 1.
19 Ibid., para. 3.
20 Roche, "Embodying Multiplicity," 115.

References

Alvin Ailey American Dance Theater. "Revelations." www.alvinailey.org/performances/repertory/revelations.

Andrade, Luis M., and Robert Gutierrez-Perez. "Bailando Con las Sombras: Spiritual Activism and Soul Healing in the War Years." *Qualitative Inquiry*, vol. 23, no. 7, 2017, pp. 502–504.

Deleuze, Giles. *Difference and Repetition*. 1968. Translated by Paul Patton, Columbia UP, 1994.

Greene, Maxine. *Releasing the Imagination: Essays on Education, the Arts, and Social Change*. Jossey-Bass, 1995.

Hofesh Shechter Company. "Our Story." www.hofesh.co.uk/about-us/our-story/.

Kristeva, Julia. *Intimate Revolt*. 1997. Translated by Jeanine Herman. Columbia UP, 2003.

Mackrell, Judith. "Interview: 'War Was Coming Through the Window.'" *The Guardian*, 11 Jan. 2009, www.theguardian.com/stage/2009/jan/12/dance-hofesh-shechter-choreographer.

Markula, Pirkko. "Body-Movement-Change: Dance as Performative Qualitative Research." *Journal of Sport and Social Issues*, vol. 30, no. 4, 2006, pp. 353–363.

Milford Graves Full Mantis. Directed by Jake Meginsky, performances by Milford Graves, Mantis Film, 2018.

Moelwyn-Hughes, Lucy, et al. *Barbarians: A Trilogy by Hofesh Shechter. Resource Pack for Students and Teachers*. Hofesh Shechter Company, 2017.

Monnier, Mathilde, and Jean-Luc Nancy. "Alliterations," translated by Noémie Solomon. *Perform, Repeat, Record: Live Art in History*, edited by Amelia Jones and Adrian Heathfield. Intellect Books, 2012, pp. 595–602.

Reynolds, Dee. "A Technique for Power: Reconfiguring Economies of Energy in Martha Graham's Early Work." *Dance Research*, vol. 20, no. 1, 2002, pp. 3–32.

Roche, Jenny. "Embodying Multiplicity: The Independent Contemporary Dancer's Moving Identity." *Research in Dance Education*, vol. 12, no. 2, 2011, pp. 105–118.

Pedri-Spade, Celeste. "'The Drum is Your Document': Decolonizing Research Through Anishinabe Song and Story." *International Review of Qualitative Research*, vol. 9, no. 4, 2016, pp. 385–406.

Tsing, Anna. "The More-Than-Human Anthropocene." Unnatural Disasters: Climate Change and the Limits of the Knowable Conference, 13 Sept. 2018, Illini Union, Urbana-Champaign, IL. Keynote Address.

Ulmer, Jasmine Brooke. "*Pivots* and *Pirouettes*: Carefully Turning Traditions." *Qualitative Inquiry*, vol. 26, no. 5, 2020, pp. 454–457.

5 Simple truths

To write words that might make a difference in this world, we must be true to ourselves.

I would think if there's a concept that we'd want to be clear on in philosophy, it's truth. While I feel reasonably confident about the idea of truth in real life, as a scholar, I'm less certain about some of the ways in which truth is being taken up in research. As a qualitative inquirer, I think about this a lot amidst what has been deemed our "post-truth" era, wondering whether we are going about this in the most productive of ways. Because I'm not one to argue, my preference would have been to remain silent on this issue. Yet, when I was invited to participate on a recent conference panel on this topic, I reluctantly agreed. My sense of responsibility outweighed my discomfort with the turns we have allowed—and even encouraged—truth to take in qualitative research. It still does.

It appears to me, at least, that some branches of qualitative inquiry have been quick to decline entering into a relationship with truth. I would respectfully suggest that while this may have been well-intentioned, it has also been a mistake. As I write this, I am reminded of the first proposal I received. It was from a young man named Truth. Neither one of us was ready for marriage then. First, we weren't in a relationship. Second, we weren't old enough to get married, let alone drive. Which is why the proposal took place one afternoon on a big, yellow school bus. After talking it through a little bit more, it became apparent that we had incompatible visions of marriage, and we concluded that getting hitched probably wasn't going to be the best of ideas—even if he did eventually want to go on a two-year mission and have a fiancé or a wife to write letters home to while he was away. Yet, it's one thing to say that I wasn't ready to commit to a life-long relationship with Truth the person; it's another thing to say that, as a researcher or as a person in this world, I'm unwilling to be in a meaningful, long-term relationship with the general concept of truth today.

These times call for a return to truth in qualitative inquiry. Kuntz, for example, notes that certain approaches to methodology have been reluctant "to invoke the term 'truth' or 'truths' for fear of essentializing or underdetermining experience, inference, or some elements of confected reality."[1] Accordingly, he continues, inquirers have moved so far away from truth-telling that

> we have achieved a type of methodologically induced paralysis— we've no truths upon which to act (or a landscape of multiple, overdetermined truths, the multiplicity of which makes it impossible for us to act). In this way methodologically informed relativism has a hand in the normalization of collective docility. We cannot remove ourselves from a shared responsibility for such consequences.[2]

We have been the ones, Kuntz observes, to open the door to contradictory truths and nontruths. It is disturbing that in the short time since his book *The Responsible Methodologist* was published, "alternative facts," "fake news," and "post-truth" have all been added to our daily lexicon.

It is within this spirit of truth-telling that I joined the symposium panel,[3] grateful for the opportunity to refine my own thinking—not to dissect where we went astray, but to shift toward where we have already gotten it right. The brief remarks I expressed on this panel appear below. I would share that they were influenced by writings of bell hooks and Grace Lee Boggs, both of whom maintain a keen focus on what's important in difficult times. I also appreciate being able to write with the advice of Martin Luther King, Jr., who offers two reassurances that I find particularly relevant. The first reminds us not only to speak, but to "speak with all the humility that is appropriate to our limited vision."[4] The second presciently addresses inclinations to get stuck within relativist frames. As King recommends, "We are always on the verge of being mesmerized by uncertainty. But we must move on."[5] I hope to illustrate how we might do this here.

"The truth is"

We've been asked to reconsider qualitative research in what many now refer to as a "post-truth" era. As a qualitative methodologist who believes that the different methodologies we use may have the potential to manufacture different truths, I take this task quite seriously.

What seems to be underneath these sorts of methodological reckonings are questions of, what is truth? Who has truth? Who gets to share, discover, make, and tell these truths? Although these questions are not new, nowadays, notions of truth seem to be increasingly complicated.

Except, I'm not so sure they are. But I'll come back to this.

Recently, The Cause Collective[6] travelled to different sites throughout Detroit and Flint, Michigan. They carried with them an inflatable recording studio, some cameras, and three small, yet powerful, words: "the truth is." These three words were a prompt—an invitation—an opening for passersby to enter the booth and express their own truths in two minutes or less.

Now, as methodologists, many of us are trained to be suspicious of anyone who offers to tell us the truth, particularly when they believe they can accomplish this in two minutes or less. More broadly, however, we are trained as scholars to pick apart and be skeptical of anything that happens to resemble truth. For good reason, nuance is often much of what we do. Yet, instead of two-minute riffs in an inflatable recording studio, we regularly attempt to communicate scholarly truths over, say, the course of 10- to 15-minute symposium remarks and 6,000-word articles (meanwhile expressing potential truths we hope our respective methodological discourse communities might find palatable). In other words, given relatively short amounts of time and space, we as scholars have the ability to complicate—or problematize—things rather quickly.

Arguably, society encourages this. How often do we see media organizations offering analyses that claim to fact-check political speeches and remarks, listing the number of total falsehoods alongside calculations of what percentage of truth someone might be telling in order to, really, when it comes right down to it, call someone a liar? By continuing to respond to what is not true, we can become caught in endless feedback loops and toxic uses of time and energy. This, as many might agree, can be exhausting, if not dispiriting.

The search for political truth can spiral into competitions for the best truths, the most effective and compelling truths, the sexiest, flashiest, and most memorable truths, or, in keeping with Stephen Colbert, the "truthiest" truths. Yet, just as truth is not a superlative or percentage, "the truth is" involves more than a passing prompt: those three particular words—"the truth is"—form a complete sentence in and of themselves.

As such, I wonder why we so often look outward to politicians, public figures, and news media organizations as arbitrators of the truth. In other words, why look to others to narrate the truth when we instead could be looking inward at ourselves for the truths we already possess?

Specifically, what I'm wondering, then, is whether we perhaps have become so focused on what is *not* true that we have forgotten to hold on to what actually is—to what has the potential to be real and true and is already in front of us. And what I am proposing, then, is this: to consider setting aside the "games of truth"[7] we sometimes play in methodology, and instead redirect our limited time and energies in educational research—or at least *some* of them—to revisiting what is true, what might be true, or what might one day become true. I would hope there is still a place for such lines of thinking within and across the varied branches of methodology, regardless of whether their respective relationships with facts and truth are approached as singular, plural, situated, partial, objective, subjective, multiple, constructed, or something else entirely.

Yet, truth isn't just something that we find, uncover, or describe through methodology. Rather, truth is a discourse in and of itself, or, perhaps more accurately, a series of discourses. Some may be theoretical. Others may be epistemological, ontological, or philosophical. Regardless of which discourses we invoke, however, the myriad perspectives from which we draw inform not only the different types of truths we share, but how, in turn, they are narrated.

This is important because truth is something that is narrated. Though we often think of narration as a fictional device, truth has the structure of fiction insofar as it is narrated. To quote Jacques Lacan, truth "*comes out*, but that isn't enough. *It speaks.* It says things, usually things we were not expecting."[8] As he writes in *My Teaching*, the truth comes out through narration, particularly when we narrate the stories of our lives. These stories may not form *objective* truths, but narrations of *ethical* truths involving prescriptions of what we should do, what we desire, and how we should move through our lives. And to get to the larger truths within our lives, we need to narrate all of our stories together. No one person can exhaust truth within a single discourse, so we need stories from everyone at the same time. Moreover, these are not so much multiple truths as they are multiple stories about the same thing, or about the many ways to truth that course throughout our daily lives.

In explaining how, Alain Badiou positions truth as part of a multifaceted procedural ethic, one in which a particular way to truth does not stand alone but makes a necessary contribution to a collectively arrived upon truth. In other words, it is taking different paths *to* truth that allows us to arrive *at* truth. As Badiou explains in his *Manifesto for Philosophy*, these different paths to truth are political, mathematical (which we might read broadly as scientific), artistic, and amorous.[9] I'd like to point out that as qualitative researchers, we've collectively addressed all four of Badiou's truth procedures. And the truth is not one of these things by itself, but something we arrive at by working through all of these things together simultaneously. Hence, it is not that we as researchers need to respond to all the truth procedures at once, but to recognize that they exist, even if we only focus on one or two in our work.

For me, then, the truth is not as complicated as we sometimes make it in methodology or research. This is not to suggest that the truth is inherently simple. Oftentimes, the truth is anything but. Rather, what I am suggesting is that some of the most important truths can be expressed simply. Or, at least, expressed more simply than we frequently tend to do.

There are expressions of truth that are simply available—revealings of truth that make up our everyday because we are around them every day. My previous experiences as a classroom teacher make this clear. As a result, my own work happens to pull truth from love, as, again, I am interested in the potential of expressing truths more simply. To illustrate, I'll now join others in Detroit and Flint who have narrated some of the truths within their lives. So, in two minutes or less, along with a photograph I took on the day of the panel, here is mine.

Children already know the truth

I may be a qualitative research methodologist now, but I began as a public school elementary teacher. I enjoyed teaching children, conversing with children, and, in the process, learning more from them than perhaps they ever did from me. And one of the very most important things I ever learned from my students was that:

> *The truth is, children already know the truth. And one of the truths children know is that for far too many reasons, far too many people do not feel heard, seen, welcome, or safe.*

From the vantage point of a child, there are times when this truth feels terrifying. Nevertheless, there are also times when it seems that children already know how to respond.

Children have an innate sense of justice. When it comes to the simplest things in life—including how people treat one another—children keenly understand what is right and what is just and what is good. Rather than being so focused on studying children or on teaching them the sorts of things that we adults think they ought to know, as educational researchers, we might change the scope of our methodological vision to consider what it is that we might *learn* from children, instead.

Children already know about truth because they are learning how to navigate the difficult inner truths of their lives every day. Few have easy paths through life, and childhoods can be interrupted all too soon. There are students at Parkland High School in Florida, for instance, who now know this all too well. This is one of many related sets of truths with which they must now live. That they deserve to be safe in schools. That clear backpacks and knowledge of CPR will not keep them safe, just as there are students in a school district in Pennsylvania who now know that keeping buckets full of rocks in classrooms to thwart potential shooters will not keep them safe, either. They know that they have been failed by the adults who could have, and should have, done more to prevent gun violence this whole time. And as students march for their lives so that they might never again experience the horrors of mass public shootings, some of their most powerful truths have been expressed in 6 minutes and 20 seconds of not only words, but silence.[10]

As children already know, a world that is safe and welcoming and listens is a world filled with simple truths. And they know that perhaps, just perhaps, the truth is not so difficult at all.

For what, at least in my own experience, so many children want most in the world is love. If we think of adults as grown children, then perhaps this is what many adults want most, as well. This has been true for so many of the children I taught then and for so many of the adults I teach now. They know that it's important to love one another. To treat others how we would want to be treated. To be welcoming. To listen and act with care and kindness in all that we do in research, in methodology, and in life.

For my students, for me, and for us together, then—the truth may be simple, but those simple truths can be so very big. In these ways, the truth is ethical, political, scientific, artistic, and also—at the same time—the truth is love.[11] This is an age, perhaps, when a little bit of love just might go a long way. Everybody needs love.

Love, then, is a simple truth—a shared truth, and perhaps the simplest truth. Children already know this, too.

Figure 5.1 Beget, 2018, New York City, New York, USA.

Qualitative truths

In the time that's followed this panel, I have since continued to think about truth and love, particularly as they pertain to qualitative inquiry. For many of us who identify as qualitative inquirers, one of our truths is likely this: we go about things qualitatively because we believe that's how things ought to be done. In adopting a qualitative axiology, it's why many of us have chosen this particular community, and it's why many of us include this community and the people in it when giving accounts of whom and what we love.

That's all to say that we *could* have chosen to go down other paths, but we didn't. We chose something else, instead. It's not that other approaches aren't needed; they are and they will continue to be. Rather, it's that we chose spaces that emerged from the many forms of inquiry we do. We chose spaces that claimed to be inclusive, yes, and also in inclusively methodological ways. We chose spaces built on promises of equity. We chose spaces that we'd hoped would support our intersectional identities and allow us to be who we are in the work we passionately go about doing every day. Not because we chose the word qualitative, necessarily, but because—through the beautiful words we were presented with—we chose the spirit it conveyed.

Beautiful words alone, however, are not enough. Even if they are positioned as beautiful words that seek to change the world, and even when they are beautiful words that we have been longing to hear. Rather than accept these words at face value, what we should do, instead, is examine how these beautiful words come into practice. Is it by exploiting the labor of scholars of color, marginalizing and profiting off those who have been doing the work? By excluding women from meaningful positions of leadership? By privileging only a select few, restricting limited opportunities in ways that maintain a White, heteronormative patriarchy? By preventing emerging scholars from entering the field? Because if the answer to any one of those questions, much less *all* of them, is yes, then those spaces aren't what they've been claiming to be, and we shouldn't be a part of them. We shouldn't be a part of spaces that operate without honesty, transparency, or responsibility, attempting to dominate and control others through fear. Instead, we should reexamine who and what we've been called to resist. When we are not careful with our time and energy and money and publications and citational practices, we can inadvertently reinforce the inequitable systems that we have been aiming to work against. If we instead decided to work in solidarity to create other options—ones that actually are what they claim to be—then we could begin to operate differently. It's a challenge, to be sure. At the same time, it is also within reach. We can do the work to make it happen and help others do the same.[12]

When we share and collaborate in real and genuine ways, it becomes possible to create the spaces that we want to be in. To do so, we have to be willing to let go of that which no longer serves us (and may not have ever served us to begin with). When we are not aware that beautiful words are being put in place to cover ugly practices, we can end up being blindsided by those who are in it for the wrong reasons—by those who have learned to co-opt the words of others solely for themselves. Even words such as collaboration and sharing are not immune. We cannot fix what has already been broken and corrupted beyond repair, and nor should we continue to try.

As people, we have moral and ethical obligations to one another. When we fail to recognize and elevate those around us, we have failed. We have failed to listen. We have failed to see. We have failed to act with humanity toward our fellow human beings. And we have failed to bring into being what this is supposed to be.

Qualitative research wasn't a term in my grandfather's dictionary. It has gone by other names before, and it may go by other names still, but here's what I think will continue to hold: truths involving people are deeper truths, and those truths have the ability to spark profound and lasting change. At its best, qualitative inquiry treats people as people. And when we do just that, we can begin to manifest the potential of who we are and what we can accomplish together.

Notes

1 Kuntz, *The Responsible Methodologist*, 98.
2 Ibid., 98.
3 Ulmer, "Adjusting the Scope of Methodological Vision," n.p.
4 King, "Beyond Vietnam," para. 4.
5 Ibid., para. 3.
6 Cause Collective, "The Truth Is I Hear You," para. 1.
7 Foucault, *Subjectivity and Truth*, 221.
8 Lacan, *My Teaching*, 15.
9 Badiou, *Manifesto for Philosophy*, 141.
10 Reilly, "Emma González Kept America in Stunned Silence," para. 3.
11 Boggs and Kurashige, *The Next American Revolution*, 47; hooks, *All About Love*, 4.
12 See St.Pierre, "Post Qualitative Inquiry, the Refusal of Method, and the Risk of the New," 5.

References

Badiou, Alain. *Manifesto for Philosophy*. 1989. Translated by Norman Madarasz, SUNY Press, 1992.

Boggs, Grace Lee, and Scott Kurashige. *The Next American Revolution: Sustainable Activism for the Twenty-first Century*. University of California Press, 2012.

The Cause Collective. "The Truth Is I Hear You: A Project By The Cause Collective." http://cranbrookartmuseum.org/exhibition/the-truth-is-i-hear-you/.

hooks, bell. *All About Love: New Visions*. HarperCollins, 2000.

Foucault, Michel. *Subjectivity and Truth: Lectures at the Collège de France, 1980–1981*. Translated by Graham Burchell, Palgrave Macmillan, 2017.

King, Martin Luther, Jr. "Beyond Vietnam." The Martin Luther King, Jr. Research and Education Institute, 4 April 1967, https://kinginstitute.stanford.edu/king-papers/documents/beyond-vietnam.

Kuntz, Aaron. *The Responsible Methodologist: Inquiry, Truth-Telling, and Social Justice*. Left Coast Press, 2015.

Lacan, Jacques. *My Teaching*. Translated by David Macey, Verso, 2008.

Reilly, Katie. "Emma González Kept America in Stunned Silence to Show How Quickly 17 People Died at Parkland." *Time Magazine*, 4 Mar. 2018, https://time.com/5214322/emma-gonzalez-march-for-our-lives-speech/.

St.Pierre, Elizabeth Adams. "Post Qualitative Inquiry, the Refusal of Method, and the Risk of the New." *Qualitative Inquiry*, advance online publication, 2020.

Ulmer, Jasmine Brooke. "Adjusting the Scope of Methodological Vision." In "Alternative Facts, Fake News, and Educational Research: Reconsidering Qualitative Methodologies," chaired by Robert Donmoyer. Annual meeting of the American Educational Research Association, 15 April 2018, New York, NY. Symposium.

6 Everyday invitations
A photographic interlude

Figure 6.1 Unplug, 2018, Groningen, the Netherlands.

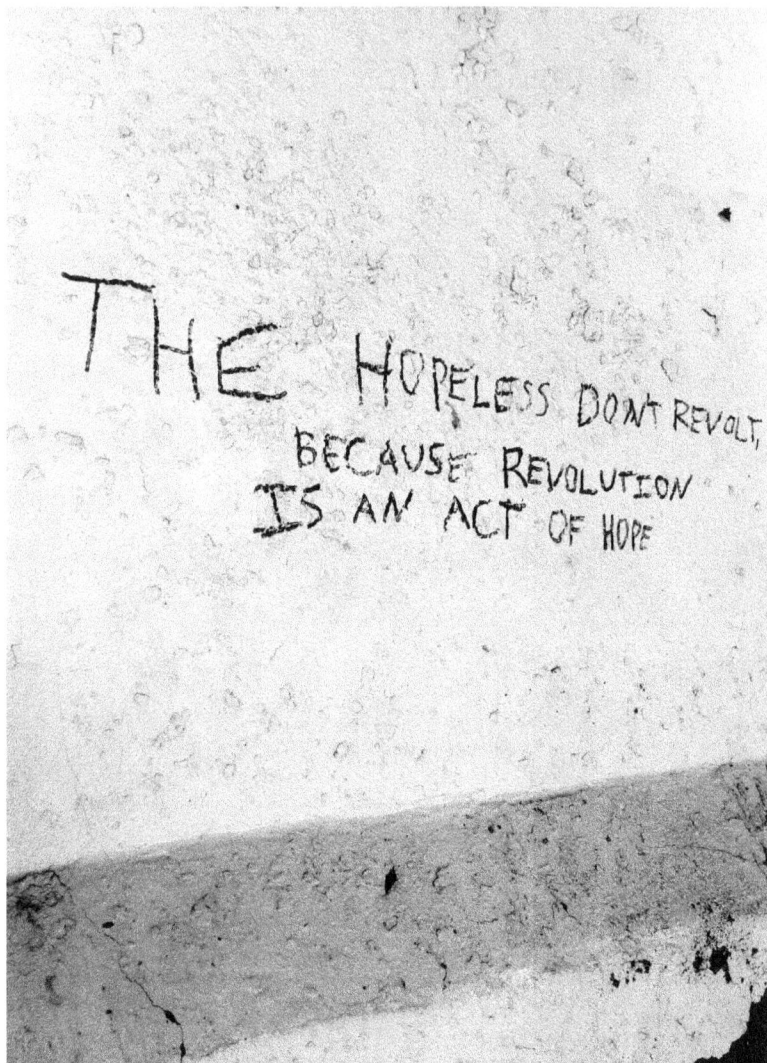

Figure 6.2 Hope, 2017, Detroit, Michigan, USA.

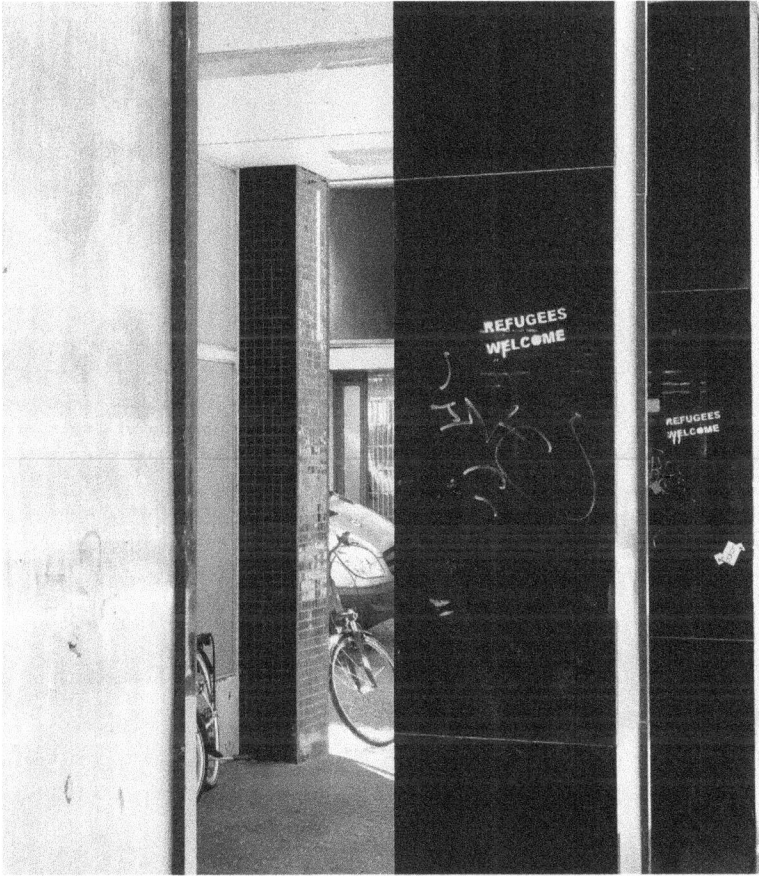

Figure 6.3 Welcome, 2018, Leiden, the Netherlands.

Figure 6.4 Love, 2017, Detroit, Michigan, USA.

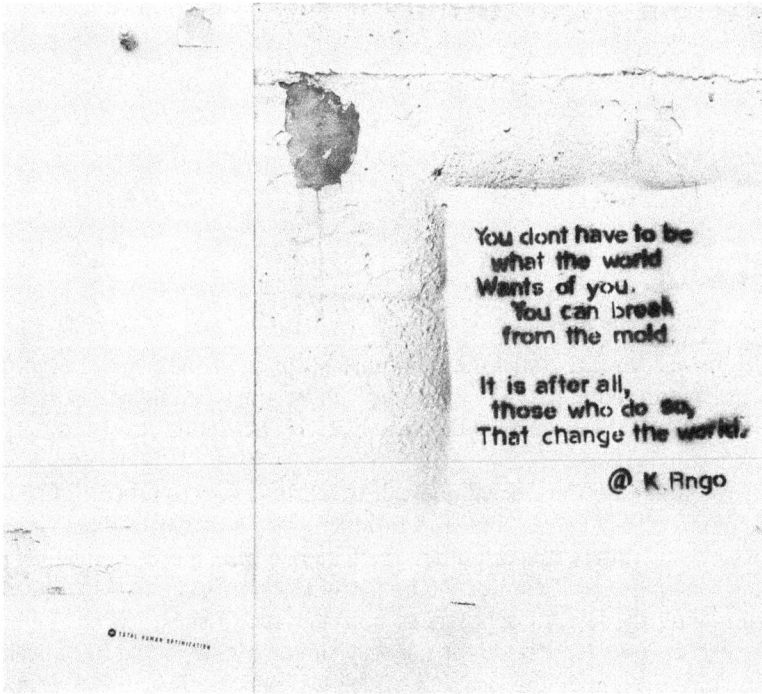

Figure 6.5 Change, 2017, Detroit, Michigan, USA.

7 Tiny revolutions

To move forward, sometimes we must go back to the beginning and start again. This, perhaps, is one of those times. Amidst the backdrop of constant change, the fragilities of academia are becoming increasingly clear.

For many, this has raised questions regarding how to proceed. From critiques of academic labor and production to speculative imaginings of new and different possibilities, the focus on what might happen next has been pressing. I am not the first, and sincerely hope that I will not be among the last, of scholars to consider such issues. I would offer an expression of gratitude for the very smart thinkings that have been previously offered, the ways in which we benefit from the wisdom within them, and the thinkings and teachings yet to come. Shared challenges need shared solutions and ideas: these are matters of collective sustainability.

I have been wondering, then, whether the question of *how* to proceed in academia perhaps has begun to shift into a question of *if* we can proceed. And, moreover, if this potential future (or set of futures) is possible, I wonder if it (or they) will materialize in a form that would be recognizable to us now, much less recognizable to us at the end of our careers. In other words, the principles underlying questions of how academia might go about doing something are different from questions considering if academia, at least as we know it, will continue to exist. This is because *if* is a separate, albeit related, question—one that reflects an ongoing wave of displacements within higher education. From the counting and commodification of intellectual thoughts to the shrinking number of opportunities that are available to guide and support these endeavors, the future can seem precarious. In the many aspects of our day-to-day work as inquirers, we are not exempt from the ways in which the broader academic landscape continues to change. This is why I choose to approach the question of *if* through *how*. It provides a frame for addressing the question I ask here, which is: If the best parts of academic practice can continue to exist, how might they hold together? Or, put most simply: *And if, then how?*

As I write this, I find myself nostalgic for futures that have not yet arrived, even as I recognize that nostalgia typically is reserved for past experiences. To say that I read future potentialities through nostalgia may seem a bit strange, or, at least it does for me. If I am indeed to hinge upon the *if*—as I do here in this chapter—then I am forced to contend with the full range of possibilities. As scholars, there are times when we take up possibilities as proxies for hopes and desires. When this happens, we write what we hope will become possible as if, in fact, it was possible to write ourselves and the futures we desire into existence. Perhaps it is. What feels less satisfying to write about, however, are the potential impotentialities—the possible impossibilities. And though, as scholars, we might know what we want and what feels right, I would be remiss if I did not mention that, given the various material existences in which we find ourselves thrown, we may be faced with *impossibilities*, as well. Simply wanting something is not enough in and of itself; alone, desire is insufficient. When Tinker Bell's light fades after she drinks the poison intended for Peter Pan, the audience revives her by applauding and believing in fairies. Yet, we cannot collectively bring a fictional fairy back to life any more than we can recreate academic pasts that no longer seem to exist. This is unlikely to change, however much we might mourn for what already has been lost, feel anxious about today and tomorrow, or wistfully yearn for the futures that might once have been there for others, but likely will not continue to be there for the scholars who are just starting now.

I take great comfort, however, in knowing that we are not alone. As an avid reader, I have stacks and stacks of books on my shelves. So even in the midst of tumultuous and troubled times, there is always wisdom from others to be found. Others who, in fact, lived through different— yet very much related—sets of troubled and tumultuous times themselves. Others in the field who not only overcame challenges and made contributions of their own but cleared the path so that we may do the work we feel compelled to do today. Although there are times when we must go back to the beginning and start again—and I would suggest that this is indeed one of them—we need not erase what has already been done. In other words, this does not mean that we must mindlessly repeat what has already been done simply because it has been done before, but that we should build upon what has already been learned as we respond to the troubles of today.

This is another moment in which we seem to be "arriving where we started."[1] And in the journey back to where we began, many histories have been told, many suggestions have been made, and many lessons have been learned. There is much we should be sure not to forget.

At the same time, we should carefully turn tradition where necessary and not remain too caught up in what has been done before. In taking up the philosophy of abundance in *Where Do We Go from Here: Chaos or Community?*, Martin Luther King, Jr. expressed that, "We are wasting and degrading human life by clinging to archaic thinking."[2] When we build and maintain shared communities through a philosophy of abundance, both in times of real and perceived scarcity, we put the generations that will follow in a better position to succeed. This continues to be necessary because, as he wrote in a letter elsewhere, "Injustice anywhere is a threat to justice everywhere. We are caught in an inescapable network of mutuality, tied in a single garment of destiny. Whatever affects one directly affects all indirectly."[3] And although we live in uncertain times, so much of his advice continues to remain relevant, including his advice to "move past indecision to action."[4] That is important to remember, too.

The thoughts we think with and the words we write with matter, but at the end of it all, thoughts and words are not enough. There comes a point when both should lead to action—a point we arguably passed long ago. Which, of course, raises the question of how.

And if, then how?

It's a good question, I think, and it feels like the right one to ask.

I've come up with several potential responses, none of which I'll admit have been satisfying. I wrote about the lessons of moral philosophy and ethics in a popular television series, *The Good Place*. I wrote about shared and collaborative practice in education. I wrote about what we are leaving behind for future generations of children and youth with the decisions that we make today. I wrote about pure intent in the film *Children Among Men*. I wrote about Rennie Harris's dance choreography, *Exodus*. I wrote about a post in *Environment & Society* that called Paul Crutzen "Mister Anthropocene,"[5] mostly so that I could create a juxtaposition and connect back to earlier discussions of *Miss Anthropocene*. I wrote about a lot of other things, too.

I have included none of them here.

None of them felt right. Not because they weren't good ideas or I ran out of things to say or I didn't have any ideas to begin with, but because the question isn't mine to answer. Or, at least, not mine and mine alone, especially in a book on shared and collaborative practice.

And while that may seem like a convenient way to wrap up a book, it is the question that will drive what I do from here. So, for the time being, while I wait to take inspiration from you, I'll return to the simple ideas I began with in this book, which are: 1) treating people as people and 2) sharing nicely. I'll continue to carry these ideas with me, for if we were to do both of these things in a meaningful way, in community and in collaboration with one another, I believe that our practices would be radically different. I believe that the tiny revolutions they'd produce would be unstoppable. The power to do so is already within each of us.

Sometimes the things we think are most in our way are not. By way of example, I'll share a rather embarrassing story here. During the first week of our relationship—when I really, really wanted to impress him—my partner took me to a park in Urbana-Champaign, Illinois he thought I would like. Because I was fighting a migraine, I wasn't feeling well or clear-headed that day, and I probably should have had second thoughts about heading directly for the empty playground to enthusiastically swing on the swing set. I did not. I got dizzy, sat there for a good long while, and when I felt better, I held onto his arm as we slowly took a walk in the park around the lake. Because I hadn't been there before, he let me choose which way to go. We stayed on the concrete path, which was easy enough. Until, that is, we came across a gate. A gate was in the middle of the path and for a long time, I stood there staring at it, confused and unsure as to what to do. The gate was locked, we didn't have a key, and I was pretty sure that I wasn't going to be able to squeeze through it. I did figure that if I really had to, I could climb over it—I've climbed over plenty of gates and fences in my life—but that was when I was much younger and not so dizzy. I wondered if we should turn around and go back. Then, after an appropriate amount of time had passed, my partner kindly made a suggestion: "maybe we could walk around the gate."

In focusing only on the gate that blocked the path, I missed the most obvious solution, which was to simply walk around the gate. There was no connecting fence, no impassable underbrush filled with poisonous plants or dangerous creatures or hot lava or anything of the like. There weren't even any signs telling us to stay on the trail. On either side of the gate, there was only a well-worn dirt path that soon reconnected to the trail. Though we laugh about it now, it continues to serve as a useful reminder: when the path seems blocked, go around the gate.

For many of us, our paths in academia have been difficult thus far and they will be more difficult, still. We will have to use our shared resources and collective imaginations to survive. And we'll have to find creative ways of finding and reconnecting to our paths, going around the many obstacles that will be in the way. It won't be easy, but it will be worthwhile. When we do it well, the work we do as qualitative inquirers has the potential to create a better world. Small actions can have an enormous collective impact, and I am a firm believer that all that is good counts. It all makes a difference, especially when we follow a methodology of the heart.[6]

I think about these things often, because, again, I want academic life, human life, and planetary life to continue. I started to sketch these ideas out at the end of an article I wrote on the Anthropocene in *Philosophy and Theory in Higher Education* recently. It was the last piece of writing I did before beginning this book, so as a way to keep the continuity, I've included the last section of that article below.[7] In a way, it's what this book has been: an attempt to continue responding to the questions of what to do and where to begin. It's where I'll leave off here, at least for now, with the potential of little things, too.

The potential of little things, too

The Anthropocene is serious business. This is why scholars use it as a way to signal that we may be living in an epoch in which humans not only have become a force with planetary impact, but an epoch in which humanity faces extinction alongside so many other forms of life. I shudder to think about how many species of flora and fauna went extinct, acres of rainforest disappeared, and billions of tons of carbon dioxide were released into the atmosphere in even the time that it took to write this. And what exactly have I been doing about any of this? The short version of the answer is, "not enough." The longer version involves "writing about it."

It is my hope that scholarship in (and on) the Anthropocene will move beyond writing into consistently deeper perspectives on inquiry and life. That, when we choose theories that want to be used in research as much as they want to be lived across everyday material realities, we approach and engage those theories on their own terms. That we live them in ways that are generative and affirmative. That we attend to our own discourses.[8] That we ask who speaks for the future of the planet[9]... [And that we] reconsider and reconceptualize our practices. As Raewyn Connell observes, "There is always a workforce involved in the production of social-scientific knowledge."[10] That workforce would be us.

To live the Anthropocene, then—in it—through it—with anticipations beyond it—is a deeply ethical undertaking. This can be as much personal as much as it is professional, for moving with and against feelings of complacency, complicity, and desires for absolution potentially involves making many shifts, including in how we as scholars

> live teach read write act repurpose eat breathe share help engage encounter think imagine consider reimagine reconsider reciprocate give accept respond support generate regenerate restore return sustain nourish thank create affect effect impact affirm contribute become wonder question inquire philosophize.

To facilitate these types of shifts in how we move through the world, higher education is needed as much as, if not more than, ever. How we treat other humans and our in- and nonhuman companions conceivably has become something that is now much more than a moral imperative, but is necessary for existence on a planetary scale. Planetary survival is a tall order, and looking for opportunities to foster this within higher education is no small thing. Nevertheless, within higher education, there exist myriad opportunities to take up little practices that have the potential to effectuate such shifts. It can be the very smallest of actions—those that seem too humble or insignificant to matter—that perhaps end up mattering the most.

Within higher education, then, it is perhaps little, everyday kindnesses and gestures that might begin to shift the balance against academic fracking, strip mining, and other forms of scholarly extraction. Though few of us may be in an immediate position to fully escape complicity in terms of how we consume food, energy, and other gifts from the planet, we can choose to respond to the world in other ways by listening, paying attention, and uplifting those around us. All are actions we can bring to fruition in the spaces in which we already are, including within higher education. Our classrooms involve more than the teaching of content and the teaching of people: pedagogy also offers opportunities to teach and model sustaining ways of not only how we understand and exist in the world, but how we interact with others in it.

We can share kind words with academic friends, colleagues, students, and strangers, for example, just as we can be a thought partner to someone working out an idea, polishing a manuscript, or crafting a new argument. These sorts of small acts would not need to be complicated, overly involved, or even restricted to scholarly matters. Little things also might involve recycling empty water bottles abandoned in parking lots, picking up trash in the hallway or stairs to prevent others from slipping, cutting the plastic rings on six-packs of beverages to lessen the danger to sea birds and other ocean wildlife, scattering wildflower seeds across patches of dirt in the spring, planting trees, expressing appreciation, paying for the next person in line, or forming under-ground and alternative economies of generativity, friendship, and joy. They also could be as simple as smiling, saying hello, or pausing to be completely present. There are times when small amounts of care can be immeasurable for humans and nonhumans alike, particularly in a world that has the capacity to entangle everything whether it seems related or not. Actions do not have to be visible in order for them to be meaningful or to "count."

What may seem small when done alone can grow in size and scope when done together. Within the grand scheme of humanity and the even grander scheme of the planet as a whole, little things are, in fact, not so little at all. If every human were to pick up an empty water bottle off the ground and recycle it (or, if possible, forgo consuming that bottle of water altogether), then one bottle quickly could become more than eight billion bottles that were recycled or had never been used at all. Perhaps little bits of kindness might spread in similar ways and provide a form of alternative energy to continue moving forward in generative ways amidst difficult times. And while each of these would not be enough by itself, little collective actions could offer openings for ongoing works of all sizes, scales, rhythms, speeds, and magnitudes. For in the Anthropocene, we will continue to need both the little things and the big things at once. Given the state of the planet, this may be a time when we already need everything and even that may not be enough.

In closing, I am reminded of a slogan that often appears in many state and national parks: *Take nothing but pictures. Leave nothing but footprints.* It needs rethinking in the Anthropocene. We now leave footprints everywhere. We leave behind digital footprints, carbon footprints, and material footprints; we even have left footprints on the Moon. As the Anthropocene warns us, what seems small can quickly accumulate into something much larger. Yet, this warning also comes with urgent questions. Knowing what we know now, how will we produce and consume? What will we give, take, receive, and leave behind in our wake? Will we choose to commoditize the end of the world in our writings, or will we—through little practices that expand outward—move toward sustaining ways of being, living, and thinking in the world? The choices we make will be told through our writings, photographs, and footprints to the generations left to come.

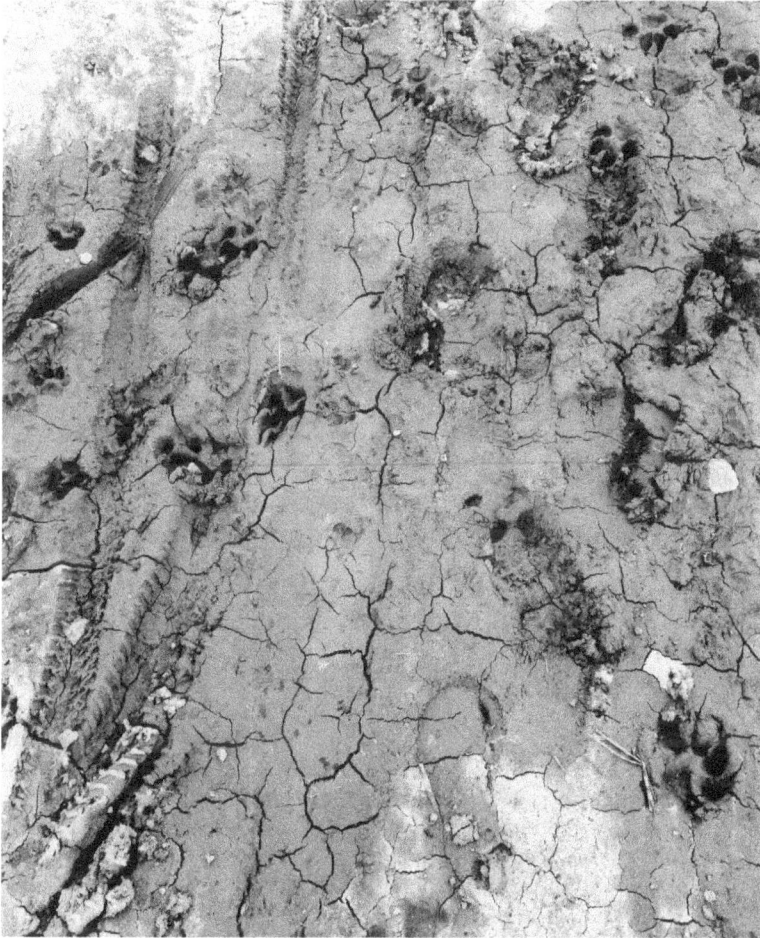

Figure 7.1 Footprints, 2017, Detroit, Michigan, USA.

Notes

1 Richardson, *Fields of Play*, 215.
2 King, *Where Do We Go From Here*, 176.
3 King, "Letter from the Birmingham Jail," 2.
4 King, "Beyond Vietnam," para. 60.
5 *Environment & Society*, Paul J. Crutzen: "Mister Anthropocene," n.p.
6 See Pelias, *A Methodology of the Heart.*
7 Section republished from Ulmer, "The Anthropocene is a Question," 79–82.
8 Gildersleeve and Kleinhesselink, "A Mangled Educational Policy Discourse Analysis," 113.
9 Lövbrand et. al, "Who Speaks for the Future of Earth?" 211.
10 Connell, *Southern Theory*, 217.

References

Connell, Raewyn. *Southern Theory: The Global Dynamics of Knowledge in Social Science*. Polity Press, 2007.
Environment & Society. "Paul J. Crutzen: "Mister Anthropocene." Environment & Society, n.d., www.environmentandsociety.org/exhibitions/anthropocene/paul-j-crutzen-mister-anthropocene.
Gildersleeve, Ryan Evely, and Katie Kleinhesselink. "A Mangled Educational Policy Discourse Analysis for the Anthropocene." In *Discursive Perspectives on Education Policy and Implementation*, edited by Jessica Nina Lester, Chad R. Lochmiller, and Rachael E. Gabriel, Palgrave Macmillan, 2017, pp. 113–132.
King, Martin Luther, Jr. "Beyond Vietnam." The Martin Luther King, Jr. Research and Education Institute, 4 April 1967, https://kinginstitute.stanford.edu/king-papers/documents/beyond-vietnam.
——. "Letter from the Birmingham Jail." 16 April 1963, http://okra.stanford.edu/transcription/document_images/undecided/630416-019.pdf.
——. *Where Do We Go from Here: Chaos or Community?* 1967. Beacon Press, 1968.
Lövbrand, Eva, Silke Beck, Jason Chilvers, Tim Forsyth, Johan Hedrén, Mike Hulme, Rolf Lidskog, and Eleftheria Vasileiadou. "Who Speaks for the Future of Earth? How Critical Social Science Can Extend the Conversation on the Anthropocene." *Global Environmental Change*, vol. 32, 2015, pp. 211–218.
Pelias, Ronald J. *A Methodology of the Heart: Evoking Daily and Academic Life.* AltaMira Press, 2004.
Richardson, Laurel. *Fields of Play: Constructing an Academic Life.* Rutgers UP, 1997.
Ulmer, Jasmine Brooke. "The Anthropocene Is a Question, Not a Strategic Plan." *Philosophy and Theory in Higher Education*, vol. 1, no. 1, 2019, 65–84.

Coda

The world is such that it is now necessary to do all of our best thinking—collectively and together—not only for the sake of humanity, but for life on the damaged planet we share. This work is, and will be, interconnected. Tiny revolutions are but a start.

I continue to have faith in what we can accomplish as qualitative inquirers, just as I continue to take heart from the following passage by Korsgaard, who writes:

> For if we human beings (1) regard ourselves as the source of our actions, and so (2) regard those actions as expressive of our selves, and at the same time (3) regard our actions as up to us, then we must regard it as up to us who and what we are. For whenever we choose our actions, we are deciding who—what sort of selves—we will be.[1]

There is much still left to decide, including who, moving forward, we will choose to be and what we will choose to do. The question of *and if, then how* is a question for you, for me, for all of us, together.

I, for one, have had enough of writing papers for the sake of writing papers and hope that there might be others who agree. With each and every passing day, there is more and more work to be done. And as James notes in the companion book *Writing & Unrecognized Academic Labor*, much of this work will be unseen.[2]

We all have limited time on this earth. To the extent we can, we should spend it carefully. I continue to believe we are capable of doing much more, and much better, than this.

Notes

1 Korsgaard, *Fellow Creatures*, 46.
2 in Salvo, *Writing & Unrecognized Academic Labor.*

References

Korsgaard, Christine Marion. *Fellow Creatures: Our Obligations to the Other Animals.* Oxford UP, 2018.
Salvo, James. *Writing & Unrecognized Academic Labor.* Routledge, 2021.

Index

Note: Page numbers in *italics* denote figures.

academia *see* scholars
accountability systems 7
Ailey, Alvin 47; *Revelations* 48
anarchy 46
Anthropocene xi, 1–2, 14, 16; Bureau
   of Linguistic Reality 25; chaos
   42; Grimes, *Miss Anthropocene*
   26–27; interaction, need for 50;
   little things, potential of 72–75;
   scope 25; Shadowtime 25; sharing
   22, 23, 24
Anzaldúa, Gloria E. xiii
Arabesque 1–4, 2018, Groningen, the
   Netherlands *31–33*
artificial intelligence (AI) 27, 34
authoritarianism 12
authors 1, 2–3; co-optation 7; ethics
   of authorship 5, 8–11; as real
   people 2, 4–7, 10; signature moving
   identities 49; *see also* writing

Badiou, Alain 56–57
Barthes, Roland 6
Beget, 2018, New York City,
   New York, USA *59*
Black, Daniel Saint, "Shadow" 25
Boggs, Grace Lee 54
Boucher, Claire Elise (Grimes), *Miss*
   Anthropocene 26–27
Bureau of Linguistic Reality, The 25

Cause Collective, The 55
change: dance 37–38; qualitative
   truths 61; revolutions 45, 46

Change, 2017, Detroit, Michigan,
   USA *67*
chaos: choreography 36, 39–42,
   47; dance-infused writing 50;
   heartbeats 40–41; revolutions 45
children: climate change 22; ethics of
   authorship 11–12; sharing 16–17;
   truth 11, 57–58
choreography 34, 36; Ailey 47; chaos
   36, 39–42, 47; connections 45;
   continuity 43; Graham 46–47;
   Monnier 48–49; returns 46–48;
   revolutions 43, 44–45; Shechter
   35, 38–40, 41–42, 45, 47, 48–49;
   see also dance
citations 24
civil rights movement 45
climate change 34; chaos 42; Grimes,
   Miss Anthropocene 26–27; post-
   truth 2; resistance 3; and sharing
   21–22, 23
Colbert, Stephen 55
collaborations 2, 13, 20; co-optation
   61; creative 24–27; dance-infused
   writing 50; tiny revolutions 71
communication: dance 38; future
   generations 12; writing as neglected
   form of 2
communities: axes of 12; continuities
   43; discourse 49, 50, 55; revolution
   50; scholarly 11, 12; shared 22–24,
   70; tiny revolutions 71
connections: choreography 45;
   revolutions 45

Connell, Raewyn 72
continuity 3, 47; dance 43; qualitative
    inquiry xii; writing 2–3, 4
creative collaborations 24–27

dance 34–35, 48; change 37–38;
    revolutions 34–36, 37, 42–46, 47,
    50; and writing 35–37, 48–50;
    see also choreography
"Dancing in the Streets", Martha
    and the Vandelas 45
dehumanization 7, 8
Deleuze, Gilles 45
democracy: and reading 18, 19;
    threats 3, 12
disconnection 2–3
discourse communities 49, 50, 55
drumming 40–41
Duncan, Isadora 46

education 3; displacements within 68;
    future generations 12; little things
    73; need for 73; *see also* scholars
elderly people, and climate change 22
extinctions 34; anthropogenic xiii;
    mass xii, 2, 12, 72

family heirlooms 17–19
Fenner, Frank xiii
Footprints, 2017, Detroit, Michigan,
    USA *75*

Graham, Martha 46–47
Graves, Milford 40–41
Greene, Maxine 34
Grimes, *Miss Anthropocene* 26–27

Hawking, Stephen xiii
heartbeats 40–41
heirlooms 17–19
historical oppressions, and climate
    change 22
Hofesh Shechter Company 35
Hofsess, Brooke 23
hooks, bell 54
Hope, 2017, Detroit, Michigan,
    USA *64*
Horton, Lester 47
Hug, 2018, Detroit, Michigan, USA *x*
humanity, shareholders in 21–22

justice 70; children's innate
    sense of 58

Kimmerer, Robin xiii
King, Martin Luther, Jr. 54, 70
Korsgaard, Christine Marion 21, 77
Kristeva, Julia 44
Kuntz, Aaron 54
Kurzweil, Ray xiii

Lacan, Jacques 56
Ladson-Billings, Gloria 10
little things, potential of 72–75
Lorde, Audre xiii
love: children 58; truth 57, 58, 60
Love, 2017, Detroit, Michigan,
    USA *66*

Markula, Pirkko 37
Martha and the Vandelas, "Dancing
    in the Streets" 45
misinformation, deliberate 1, 2
Monnier, Mathilde 48–49
Morton, Timothy 25
music 39–41

Nancy, Jean-Luc 23
narration 56
nihilism 44
Norgaard, Kari 25

oppressions, and climate change 22
Orwell, George, *Nineteen
    Eighty-Four* 3

pandemic xi
Peters, Michael A. xii–xiii
photography *x*, *14*, *31–33*, 59,
    63–67, *75*
post-truth 2, 5, 53, 54
Prince 7
propaganda 1, 3

qualitative truths 60–61

readers 1, 2; knowledge 18; as real
    people 2, 4–7
repetitions: mindless 69;
    revolutions 45–46
returns 43–44; choreography 46–48

revolts 44
revolutions xii; community 50; dance 34–36, 37, 42–46, 47, 50; tiny 14, 71, 77; writing 35–36
Reynolds, Dee 46
Roche, Jenni 48
Rotations, 2018, Ghent, Belgium *14*

Salvo, James 77
scholars 1, 2–3; Anthropocene 73; citations 24; community 11, 12; co-optation 7; dance 35, 36, 50; ethics of authorship 5, 8–11; fragilities of academia 68; future(s) of academia 68–69, 72; as real people 2, 4–7, 10; shared communities 23, 24; truth 53–57
Shadowtime 25
sharing 2, 14, 16–17; communities 22–24, 70; co-optation 61; creative collaborations 24–27; dance 34, 50; definitions 20–21, 23; ethics of authorship 12; family heirlooms 17–19; and humanity 21–22; nicely 16–17, 71; vocabulary 19–20
Shechter, Hofesh 35, 38, 45, 48; *In Your Rooms* 39–40, 41–42, 47, 48–49

Silverstein, Shel, "Prayer of the Selfish Child" 17
simple truths 58

truth: children 11, 57–58; choreography and dance 37, 48, 50; continuity 3; disconnection from 2; love 57, 58, 60; narration 56; of people 2; post-truth 2, 5, 53, 54; qualitative 60–61; scholars 53–57; simple 58; writing 37, 53
Tsing, Anna 42
Tuana, Nancy 22

Unplug, 2018, Groningen, the Netherlands *63*

vocabulary, shared 19–20

Welcome, 2018, Leiden, the Netherlands *65*
writers *see* authors
writing 1, 2–3; continuity 2–3, 4; dance-infused 35–37, 48–50; historical trajectory 2–3, 11–12; neglected as communication form 2; as a practice 9; as a privilege 11; revelations 48–50; revolutions 35–36; truth 53

For Product Safety Concerns and Information please contact our EU
representative GPSR@taylorandfrancis.com
Taylor & Francis Verlag GmbH, Kaufingerstraße 24, 80331 München, Germany